10-Inch Square Quilt Block BOOK

10-Inch Square Quilt Block Book

Landauer Publishing, *https://landauer.foxchapelpublishing.com*, is an imprint of Fox Chapel Publishing Company, Inc.

Project Team
Acquisitions Editor: Amelia Johanson
Editor: Madeline DeLuca
Proofread/Index: Gretchen Bacon
Designer: Wendy Reynolds

All photography by Carolina Moore unless otherwise noted.
Shutterstock.com photography: MaxCab (9); Deanna Laing (113).

ISBN 978-1-63981-135-9

Library of Congress Control Number: 2025939658

To learn more about the other great books from Fox Chapel Publishing, or to find a retailer near you, call toll-free 800-457-9112 or visit us at *www.FoxChapelPublishing.com.*

We are always looking for talented authors.

To submit an idea, please send a brief inquiry to acquisitions@foxchapelpublishing.com.

Or write to:
Fox Chapel Publishing
903 Square Street
Mount Joy, PA 17552

Note to Professional Copy Services:
The publisher grants you permission to make up to six copies of any quilt patterns in this book for any customer who purchased this book and states the copies are for personal use.

Printed in China
Third printing

10-Inch Square Quilt Block BOOK

40+ Quilt Patterns Using Your Favorite Pre-Cuts

Carolina Moore

Landauer Publishing

Introduction

Pre-cut 10" (25.4cm) squares are a fantastic way to make a cohesive-looking quilt with lots of variety. These sets of 10" (25.4cm) squares are all cut from the same collection of fabric, so you can feel confident that everything will coordinate beautifully. You're also able to get a variety of fabrics without having to purchase multiple individual cuts.

Easy to collect, store, and fall in love with, pre-cut 10" (25.4cm) squares are an affordable way to collect full fabric lines from your favorite designers. You may already have a shelf stacked with pre-cut fabrics waiting to be turned into quilts! Flip through the pages of this book for inspiration and instructions on how to turn these beautiful fabrics into quilts you can snuggle under.

Each quilt-top pattern in this book is made with just forty-two 10" (25.4cm) squares. You don't need additional background fabric, just a single set of pre-cut 10" (25.4cm) squares is all that you need for these quilt tops!

As you flip through your chosen fabrics, you'll get a feel for how the collection was put together. Some of these patterns work best with collections that have strong contrast, some are great for a busy collection, and some work with just about any fabric collection you choose.

Pre-cut squares are an affordable way to collect full fabric lines from your favorite designers.

Sometimes, you will find a piece of fabric in your pre-cut stack that isn't a full 10" (25.4cm) square. This is one of the ends of the bolt of fabric. Don't worry! When the fabric was cut, the ends were overlapped to ensure that you were given all your 10" (25.4cm) squares. Put this piece of fabric aside and consider it a bonus!

24
32
38
46
54
60
68
76
82
88
94
104
108

Table of Contents

Tools and Supplies

As you begin your 10" (25.4cm)-square quilt block projects, you'll want to have a few tools nearby so you're fully prepared. Because the squares are already cut to a manageable size, you don't need many supplies to turn them into quilts. Here are the basics:

Quilting Rulers

Quilting rulers are acrylic rulers with markings on them to help with accurate cutting. These can be ink markings or etched markings, depending on the brand. If you'd like to use a single ruler, the Cake Cutter Ruler was designed to work with all the quilts in this book. If you'd like to use your existing rulers, a 10" x 10" (25.4 x 25.4cm) square for trimming and squaring up, and a 3½" x 13" (8.9 x 33cm) or larger ruler for cutting down the pieces will work as well.

Marking Pen

When making half-square-triangle units, you'll want a good marking pen. Quilt shops sell chalk pencils with different colors of lead and water-soluble pens with blue ink. Both are great options. The heat-activated friction-style pens can be used on the back of fabric, but aren't recommended for the front of fabric as the ink will reappear in the cold. A simple graphite mechanical pencil is also a great option for marking on the back of fabric.

The Cake Cutter Ruler was specifically designed to work with all the quilts in this book!

Getting a rotary cutter with a fresh, sharp blade will make all the difference in your cutting.

Rotary Cutter

Combined with a quilting ruler, a rotary cutter will give clean and accurate cuts. The 45mm is the standard size for rotary cutters, although you can use a smaller or larger rotary cutter. A fresh, sharp blade will both give you cleaner cuts and be safer to use. A sharp blade requires less pressure, which gives you more control.

Cutting Mat

You'll need a self-healing cutting mat to use with the rotary cutter and ruler(s). A 24" x 24" (61 x 61cm) or larger will work best for the projects in this book. Make sure to keep heat sources away from your cutting mat—heat will warp the mat, and warped mats are unusable.

Iron and Ironing Board (or Wool Pressing Mat)

Pressing is an essential part of creating accurate quilt blocks. Having a dedicated ironing station for quilting is a luxury but not necessary. You will want to make sure that your iron is clean—a stained iron can leave unsightly stains on your quilt.

Sewing Machine

For quilting, a sewing machine with a standard straight stitch is all you need. Having a thread cutter and a needle threader on the machine is always a nice bonus. For accuracy, you may want to invest in a ¼" (6.4mm) presser foot for your machine—every brand will have this option, so check with the local sewing machine dealer for your brand. If you plan to quilt the quilts yourself, a walking foot and/or a free-motion quilting foot will be a wise investment.

When you start with pre-cuts, your tool needs are very manageable.

Check the weight of your thread before you start your project.

Thread

Many quilters prefer 100% cotton thread, but synthetic threads and blends will also work. It is important to look at the weight of the thread. The larger the number, the thinner the thread. 80–100wt thread is very fine and great for using in the bobbin. 40–50wt thread is great for piecing. Any number smaller than 40 is better suited for quilting the finished quilt than piecing.

Batting

The batting you use is a personal preference. All the quilts in this book use either 100% cotton or bamboo batting. Depending on the finished use of your quilt, wool batting, silk batting, or a batting blend (such as 80/20) could all be fantastic options.

What Are Pre-Cuts?

As the name suggests, 10" (25.4cm)-square pre-cuts come pre-cut. No need to stand at a fabric counter waiting for your fabric to be cut. You can pick your desired fabric pre-cut, purchase, and be on your way to sewing! They are already cut to size and need minimal cutting in preparation for sewing each piece together into a finished quilt!

Depending on the line of fabric used for the pre-cut pack you selected, you may find that several of the fabrics are repeated. That is because not all fabric lines have the same number of prints, but standard 10" (25.4cm)-square packs have 42 squares of fabric. Not all brands include 42 squares in their 10" (25.4cm) pre-cut packages, so double-check your packaging before you check out. You may need more than one stack of squares to complete your project.

Different brands have different names for their pre-cut fabrics. 10" (25.4cm) squares may be called a Layer Cake, 10" (25.4cm) Fabric Wonders, Ten by Tens, Stackers, 10" (25.4cm) squares, or another name.

Pre-cut 10" (25.4cm) squares in coordinated fabrics make creating quilts fun and easy.

Your pre-cut bundle could be bold colors or neutrals—there are so many fabric options!

Tips and Tricks

Before you dive in, there are some things you should consider when quilting with 10" (25.4cm) squares.

Using Pre-Cuts

Pre-cut fabric is different from fabric you have cut yourself because it is cut with a zigzag edge. When you unwrap your pre-cut fabric, you'll want to gently shake them over a trash can or outside to release any thread bits left on the edges during the cutting process. This will help keep your space tidy.

From point to point across the zigzag edges on pre-cuts is generally an accurate width, but always measure to check.

The Cake Cutter Ruler was designed for the quilts in this book, but you can also use a 10" x 10" (25.4 x 25.4cm) square ruler.

Gently flip through the fabrics to check that all the squares are whole and complete. When the squares are cut, the fabric is rolled onto long tables in tall stacks. When one roll runs out, another is added, and the start and end overlap. This overlap can result in a partial square in your pre-cut bundle. Rest assured, this is not an error, it is bonus fabric! Add it to your scrap stash for a future scrappy quilt.

Use your 10" x 10" (25.4 x 25.4cm) square ruler to measure your bundle to determine where along the edge of the bundle marks 10" (25.4cm) square. Generally, this is at the tips of the points on the zigzags. However, some bundles may have a small amount of extra fabric. In sets of 6 to 8 pieces of fabric, trim off these extra points so that you have accurate 10" (25.4cm) squares as you sew.

Do not starch pre-cut fabrics (or use similar starch alternatives). Starching and pressing fabrics can distort or shrink the fabrics. Unless you will be trimming your pre-cuts into pieces 9½" (24.1cm) square (or smaller), it is better to use them unstarched.

Making Your Own Pre-Cuts

We love pre-cuts because they are curated bundles of pre-cut fabric pieces that are virtually ready to sew! However, pre-cut bundles generally use fabric from one specific line. If you'd like to curate your own bundle from multiple lines, designers, or even multiple fabric companies, you can! You can use a quilting fabric cutter like the Accuquilt Go! or your rotary cutter and ruler to cut 10" x 10" (25.4 x 25.4cm) squares. If you're purchasing fabrics, here is a handy reference guide for how many 10" (25.4cm) squares you can cut from different cuts of fabric.

Size of fabric	Size of this fabric	Number of 10" (25.4cm) squares	How many you'll need for 42 squares
Fat quarter	18" (45.7cm) x ½ of WOF*	2	21
⅓ yard (30.5cm)	12" (30.5cm) x WOF	4	11
1 yard (91.4cm)	36" (91.4cm) x WOF	12	4

*WOF (Width of Fabric) is generally between 40" (101.6cm) and 42" (106.7cm).
Note that ½ yard (45.7cm) cuts will not yield more 10" (25.4cm) squares than a ⅓ yard (30.5cm) cut, and using smaller pieces of fabric will allow you to include a larger variety of prints in your custom pre-cut bundle.

You can also assemble your own collection! Find fabrics at the quilt shop or in your stash that you think will go well together, then cut forty-two 10" x 10" (25.4 x 25.4cm) squares. Depending on the quilt design you choose, you may want to have half light and half dark (such as the Large Half-Square Triangles quilt on page 24), or you can have a fun variety (which would look great when used to make the Quarter Log Cabin or Half Rail Fence quilts, on pages 94 and 60, respectively).

The amount of fabric you'll need to design your own collection of forty-two 10" (25.4cm) squares will vary based on the number of fabrics you use. You'd need 3¼ yards (297.2cm) if using a single fabric, but 1¾ yards (160cm) each of two fabrics. If using fat quarters, you'll need 21 total fat quarters, since you can only cut two 10" x 10" (25.4 x 25.4cm) squares from each fat quarter.

Squaring Up Blocks

Squaring up blocks is an essential step. After you finish piecing your blocks, you want to trim them to the same size so that they can easily and accurately be stitched together to make the quilt top. Not squaring up blocks may result in a quilt top that is not smooth or has puckers.

In quilting, we often refer to the "finished size" of a quilt block. The finished size is the size the block is when it is in the finished quilt. This is different from the size that you need to know when squaring up a block. Squaring up includes the seam allowances, and therefore, you square up a block to ½" (1.3cm) larger than the finished size.

If the finished size is 9" (22.9cm), square up the block to 9½" (24.1cm). If the finished size is 7½" (19cm), square up the block to 8" (20.3cm). This ensures that you have a ¼" (6.4mm) seam allowance on all four sides to piece together the blocks.

Here are the steps to squaring up*:

1. After piecing your blocks, make sure that they are well pressed and lay flat. Use a ruler the size you need or larger.

2. If you are easily distracted by too many lines on a ruler, use marking tape to mark the size you need to square up on the ruler.

* *These instructions are for right-handed quilters. For left-handed quilters, the instructions are the same, but the images would be mirrored. Left-handed quilters square up along the top and left side.*

STEP 4

STEP 5

3. Identify any reference points in the piecing of your block. The block may have diagonal seams or seams that come together in the center—these are great reference points to use when lining up the ruler.

4. Place the ruler on the quilt block. Line up any reference points. Make sure that the bottom and left edges of the block extend to or beyond the measurements for the cut size of this block.

5. Using your rotary cutter, trim away any excess fabric along the top and right side.

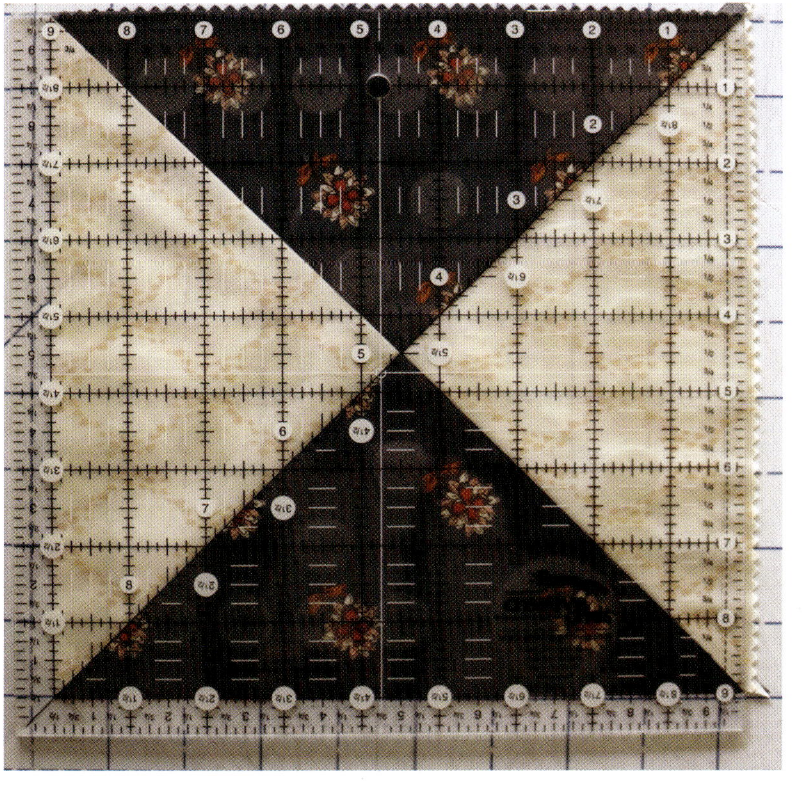

STEP 6

STEP 7

6. Lift the ruler, turn the block 180°, then place the ruler back down. Line up your reference points and line up the edges cut in the previous step with the measurements for the cut size of this block.

7. Using your rotary cutter, trim away any excess fabric along the top and right side. This will trim up the remaining two sides of the block.

8. Repeat this process for all the blocks in the quilt.

Deciding Color Placement

When purchasing a pre-cut fabric bundle, you'll have preselected fabrics that are part of a coordinating collection. While the fabrics do coordinate, you'll find a variety of dark, medium, and light values in the fabric bundle. Different collections will have different ratios of dark, medium, and light. You'll also find a variety of accent fabrics and scales of prints in different collections. This means that you could make the same pattern from this book multiple times using different fabric collections, and it would look very different each time!

Pre-cuts are designed to coordinate, but you'll still want to test color placement for your quilt pattern.

The projects in this book are colorful, vibrant, and sure to unleash your creative energy.

Many of the quilts in this book ask that you divide out fabrics by value—dark, medium, and light. Have fun with this process. Place the fabrics in piles based on what feels right. Once you've divided the fabric into piles, take a photo with your phone. Often, looking at a photo on a screen will help you more easily identify outliers in your selections. But don't worry too much about dividing up your fabrics. These patterns are very forgiving!

Projects

This collection of 42+ quilt patterns using 10" (25.4cm) pre-cuts in sets of 42 will have you going straight to the pre-cut section every time you enter your favorite fabric store. Ten-inch (25.4cm) pre-cuts are the most popular for making quilts. The bundles are cost-effective with minimal waste, they allow groupings of fabric without needing to purchase larger amounts, and they offer a good bit of fabric, enabling you to complete a beautiful quilt easily and economically. The 10" (25.4cm) size offers so many options for using as is or for cutting into blocks with minimal leftover fabric, and the coordinate prints guarantee a winning aesthetic. The designs made from these 10" (25.4cm) bundles promise something for everyone, and at all skill levels.

Large Half-Square Triangles

This quilt looks great with fabrics that can easily be divided into two contrasting piles. The blocks stitch up quickly. There are a variety of different layout options to complete your quilt top—you can make the Large Half-Square Triangles over and over again, making a completely different-looking quilt each time!

Squared-Up Block Size: 9½" (24.1cm)
Finished Block Size: 9" (22.9cm)
Finished Quilt Size: 54" x 63" (137.2 x 160cm)

Tools:

Quilting Rulers • Rotary Cutter
Cutting Mat • Iron and Ironing Board
Sewing Machine • Thread • Batting

Materials:

(42) 10" (25.4cm) squares

Instructions:

1. Divide your forty-two 10" (25.4cm) squares into two contrasting piles of 21 squares. They may be light and dark fabrics, or they can be divided into two colors, such as reds and blues, depending on the pre-cut fabric bundle you've chosen.

2. Select one pile. This is Pile 1. The remaining pile is Pile 2. Draw a diagonal line on the back of each of the squares in Pile 1.

3. Pair each square in Pile 1 with a square in Pile 2. Place them right sides together and stitch ¼" (6.4mm) away from each side of the drawn line.

4. Cut on the drawn line. Open each half and press toward the dark color.

5. This will make 42 half-square triangle units.

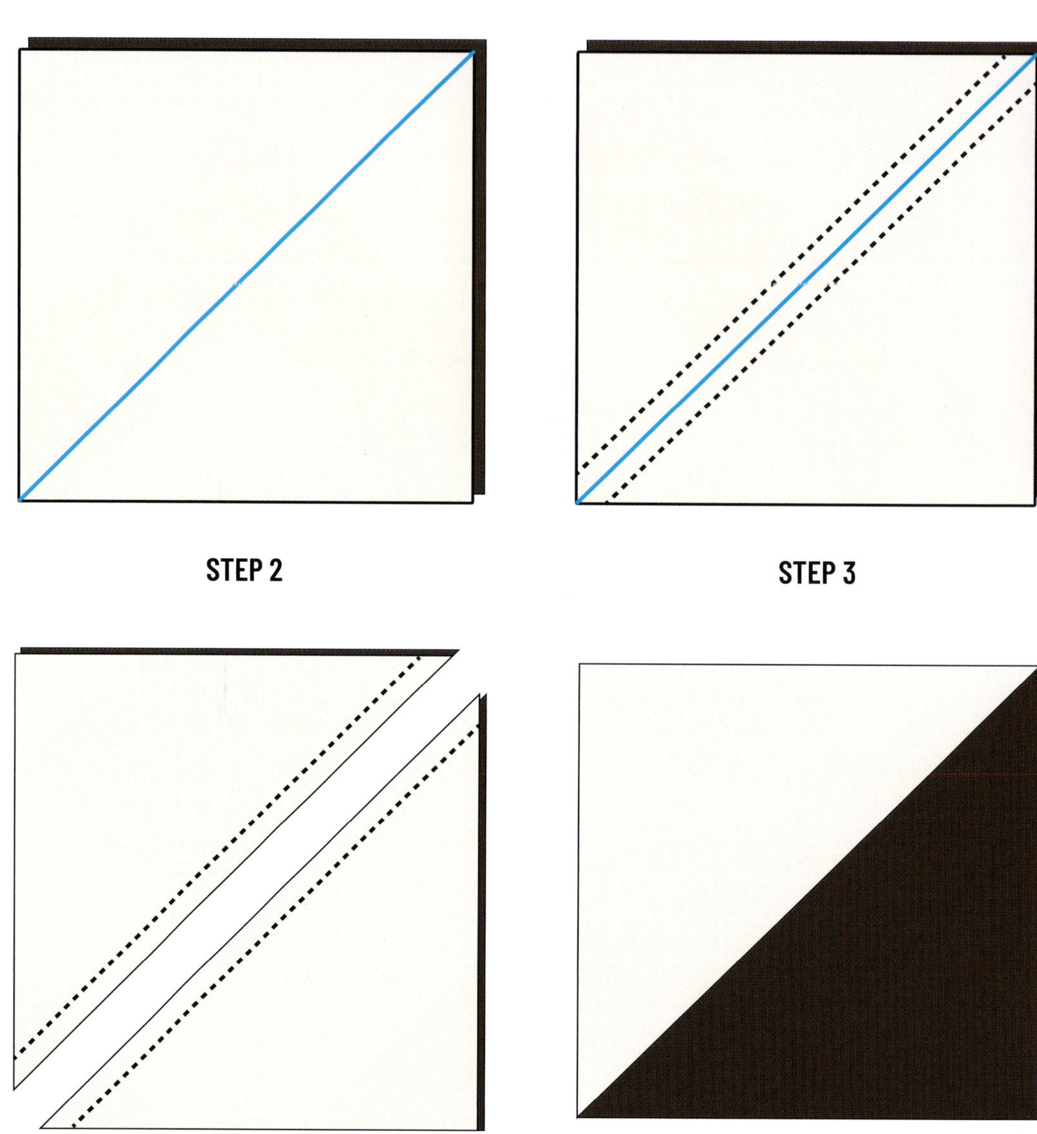

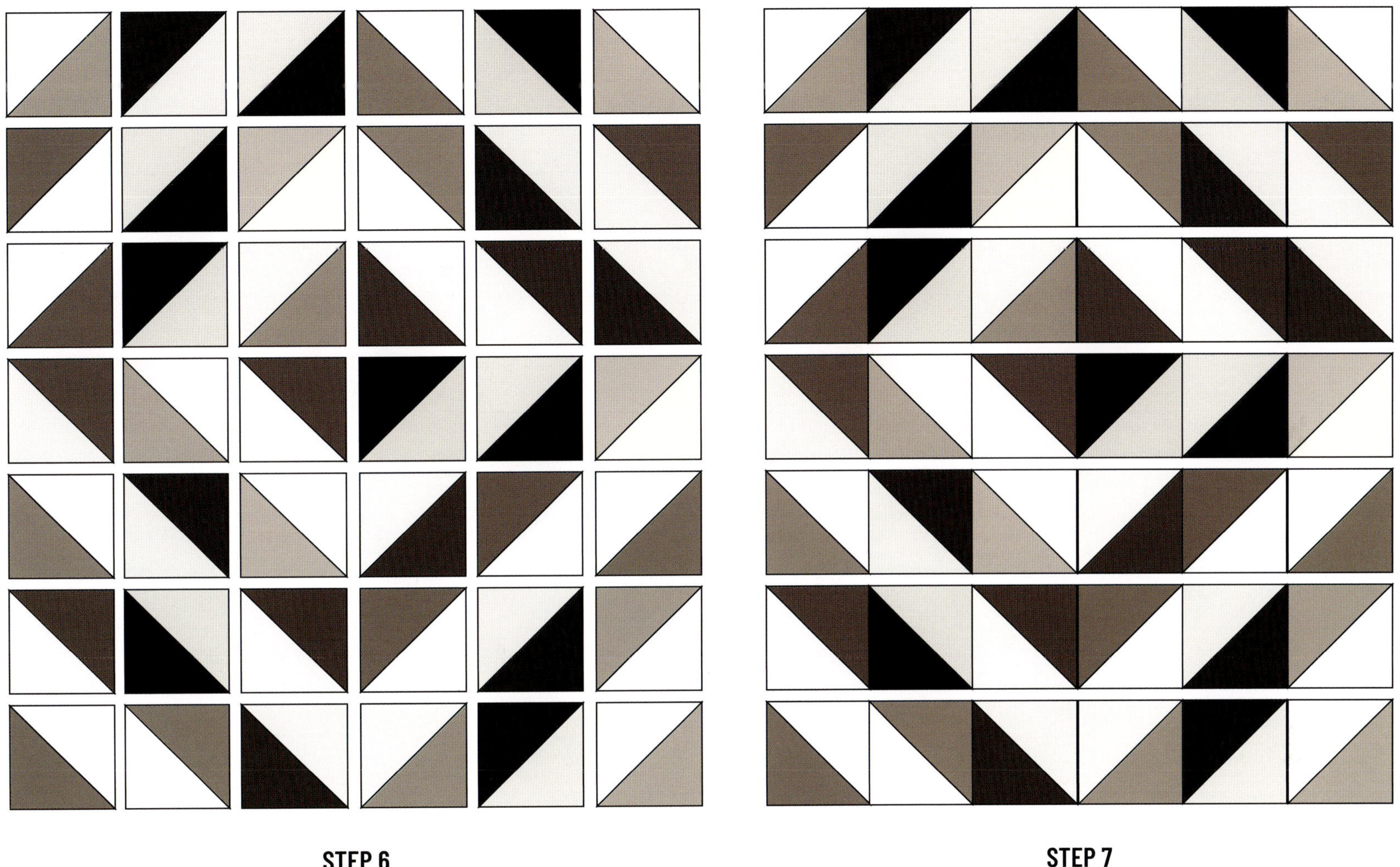

6. Lay out your half-square triangle units in the desired configuration. See the layout options on pages 29 to 31.

7. Stitch the blocks into rows. Press the seams in alternating directions.

STEP 8

8. Stitch the rows together. Press the seams in one direction.

9. Quilt and bind as desired. See the sections on quilting and binding starting on page 117 for more ideas.

Layout Options

Each layout offers a different take on the quilt design. Follow one exactly, or let it guide your improvisation.

LAYOUT OPTION 1: NESTED DIAMONDS

LAYOUT OPTION 2: FALLING ARROWS

LAYOUT OPTION 3: DIAGONAL DRIFT

LAYOUT OPTION 4: ZIGZAGS

LAYOUT OPTION 5: TRIANGLE TANGLE

Simple Four-Patches

These four-patches make a great simple sewing project for a beginner. Simple to cut and easy to sew together, you'll return to this pattern again and again when you need a quick quilt that looks lovingly handmade.

Squared-Up Block Size: 9½" (24.1cm)
Finished Block Size: 9" (22.9cm)
Finished Quilt Size: 54" x 63" (137.2 x 160cm)

Tools:

Quilting Rulers • Rotary Cutter
Cutting Mat • Iron and Ironing Board
Sewing Machine • Thread • Batting

Materials:

(42) 10" (25.4cm) squares

Instructions:

1. Divide the 42 squares in your precut bundle into three piles. One pile will have 10 dark fabrics, one pile will have 10 light fabrics, and one pile will have 20 medium fabrics (you will have two extra).

2. Square up the medium fabric pieces to 9½" (24.1cm). Set aside.

3. Cut each of the dark and light fabric squares into four squares, each 5" x 5" (12.7 x 12.7cm). You'll do this by cutting them in half vertically, and then horizontally.

4. Sew the 5" (12.7cm) squares into pairs of one dark and one light as shown. Press toward the dark fabric.

STEP 3

STEP 4

5. Sew each of the pairs to another pair, making a four-patch. Press seams in one direction or spin the seams.

6. Each four-patch can be squared up to 9½" (24.1cm) squares.

7. Lay out the blocks as shown. Alternate the un-pieced 9½" (24.1cm) units with the four-patch units.

STEP 5

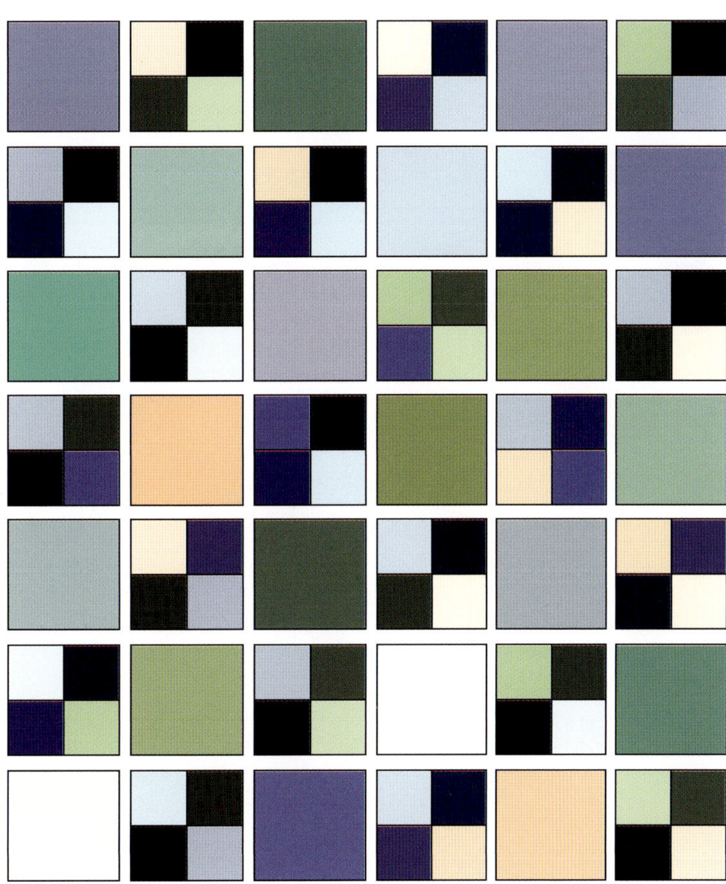

STEP 7

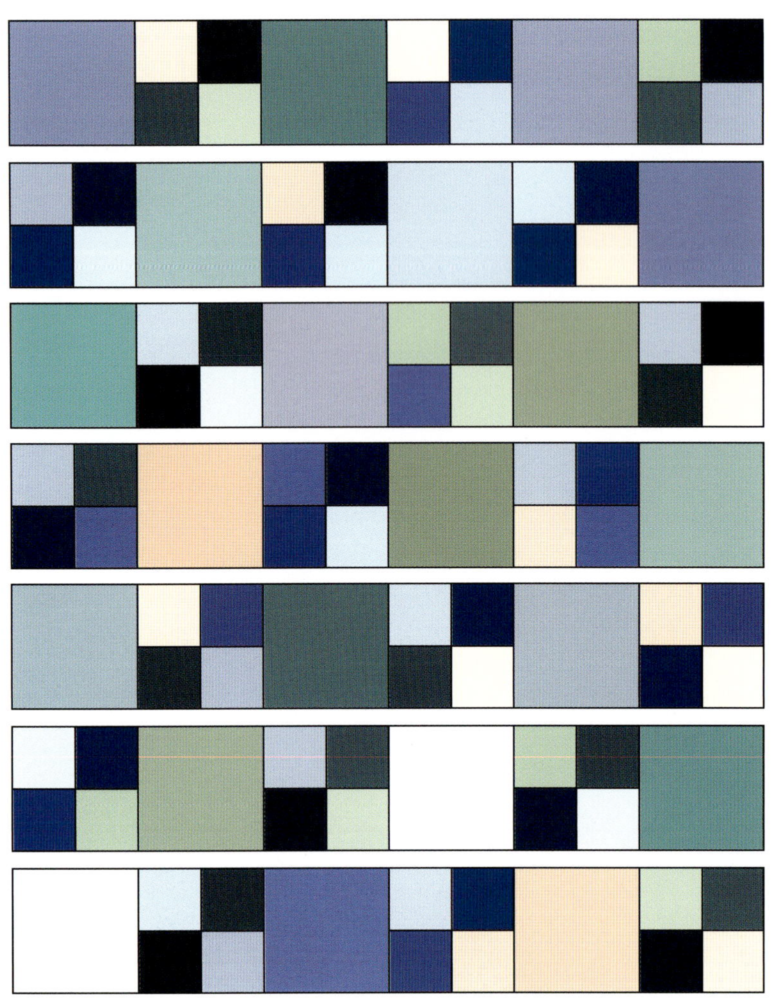

STEP 8

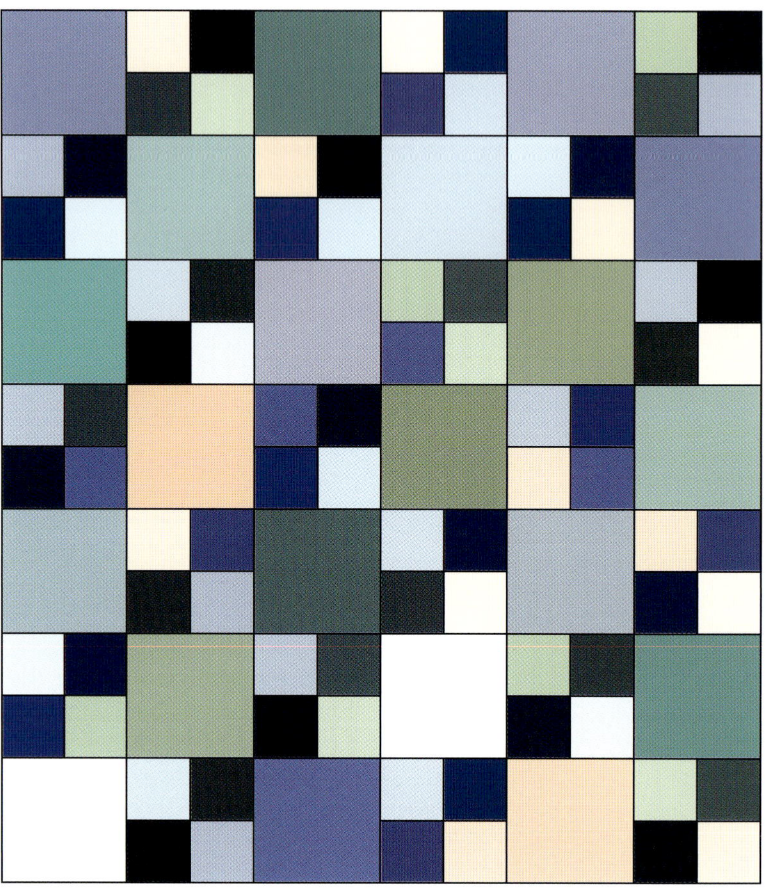

STEP 9

8. Stitch into rows. Press toward the unpieced units.

9. Stitch the rows together to make the quilt top. Press the seams in one direction.

10. Quilt and bind as desired. See the sections on quilting and binding starting on page 117 for more ideas.

Layout Options

Alternatively, divide and cut all 42 squares into four 5" x 5" (12.7 x 12.7cm) squares. Sew into four-patches as described in the step-by-step. Square up, then stitch together for a scrappier-looking quilt.

LAYOUT OPTION 1: PATCHWORK ECHO

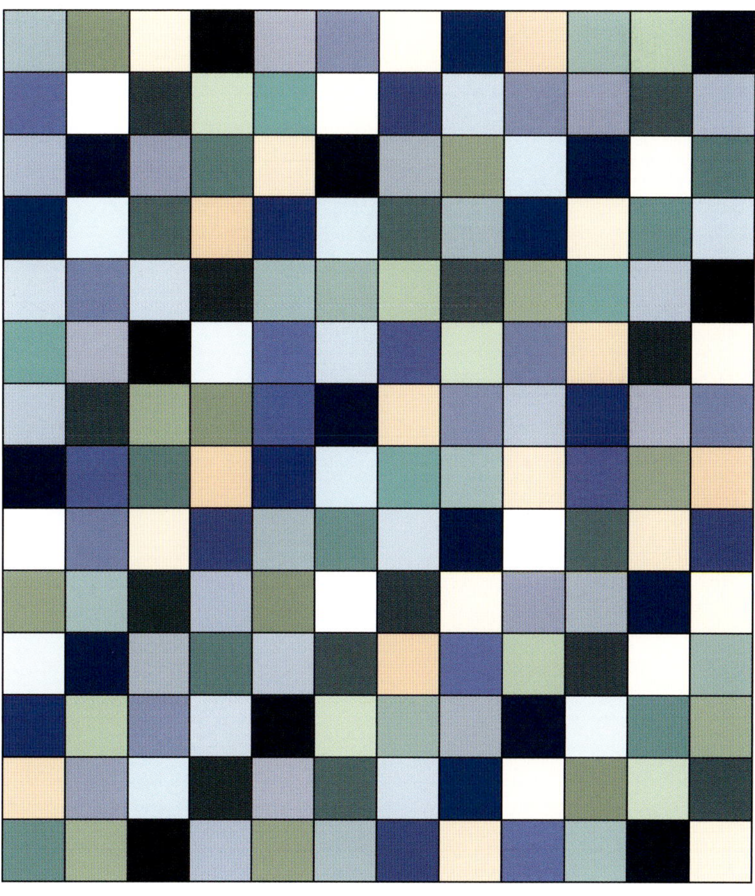

LAYOUT OPTION 2: PIXEL PATCH

Smaller Half-Square Triangles

This quilt will take more time than the Large Half-Square Triangles, but it gives such a fun and scrappy look, it is worth the extra sewing! With plenty of design options to complete the quilt top, you'll find lots of excuses to make this quilt.

Squared-Up Block Size: 4½" (11.4cm)
Finished Block Size: 4" (10.2cm)
Finished Quilt Size: 48" x 56" (122 x 142.2cm)

Tools:

Quilting Rulers • Rotary Cutter
Cutting Mat • Iron and Ironing Board • Marking Pens
Sewing Machine • Thread • Batting

Materials:

(42) 10" (25.4cm) squares

Instructions:

1. Divide your forty-two 10" (25.4cm) squares into two contrasting piles of 21 squares. They may be light and dark fabrics, or they can be divided into two colors, such as reds and blues, depending on the pre-cut fabric bundle you've chosen.

2. Cut each of the 10" (25.4cm) squares into four 5" x 5" (12.7 x 12.7cm) squares. You'll now have 81 smaller squares in each of the two piles.

3. Select one pile. This is Pile 1. The remaining pile is Pile 2. Draw a diagonal line on the back of each of the squares in Pile 1.

4. Pair each square in Pile 1 with a square in Pile 2. Place them right sides together and stitch ¼" (6.4mm) away from each side of the drawn line.

STEP 2

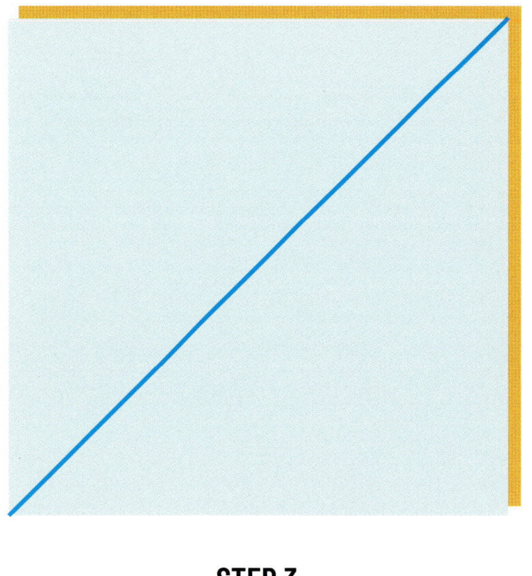

STEP 3

STEP 4

5. Cut on the drawn line. Open each half and press toward the dark color.

6. This will make 168 half-square triangle units.

7. Lay out your half-square triangle units in the desired configuration. See the diagrams on pages 43–45 for examples.

STEP 5

STEP 6

STEP 7

STEP 8

STEP 9

8. Stitch the blocks into rows. Press the seams in alternating directions.

9. Stitch the rows together. Press the seams in one direction.

10. Quilt and bind as desired. See the sections on quilting and binding starting on page 117 for more ideas.

Layout Options

Each layout offers a different take on the quilt design. Follow one exactly, or let it guide your improvisation.

LAYOUT OPTION 1: ZIPPY CHEVRONS

LAYOUT OPTION 2: SLANTWISE

LAYOUT OPTION 3: BOLD BOUNCE

LAYOUT OPTION 4: PATCH PRISM

LAYOUT OPTION 5: SCRAPPY ARROWS

LAYOUT OPTION 6: CRISSCROSSED

Snowball Corners Blocks

Adding the snowball corners to the blocks is a great beginner sewing project—you sew on the lines, and don't need to worry about a perfect ¼" (6.4mm) seam allowance. This quilt is great for fabrics that have large focal prints you don't want to cut down into smaller pieces.

Squared-Up Block Size: 10" (25.4cm)
Finished Block Size: 9½" (24.1cm)
Finished Quilt Size: 47.5" x 47.5" (120.7 x 120.7cm)

Tools:

Quilting Rulers • Marking Pens • Rotary Cutter
Cutting Mat • Iron and Ironing Board
Sewing Machine • Thread • Batting

Materials:

(42) 10" (25.4cm) squares

Instructions:

1. Divide your forty-two 10" (25.4cm) squares into two contrasting piles, one with 25 squares and the other with 13 squares. They may be light and dark fabrics, or they can be divided into two colors, such as reds and blues, depending on the pre-cut fabric bundle you've chosen (you'll have four left over).

2. Set the larger pile aside.

3. Cut each of the 13 squares into four squares, each 5" x 5" (12.7 x 12.7cm). You'll do this by cutting them in half vertically, and then horizontally.

4. With a fabric-marking pen, draw a diagonal line on the back of each of the 5" x 5" (12.7 x 12.7cm) squares.

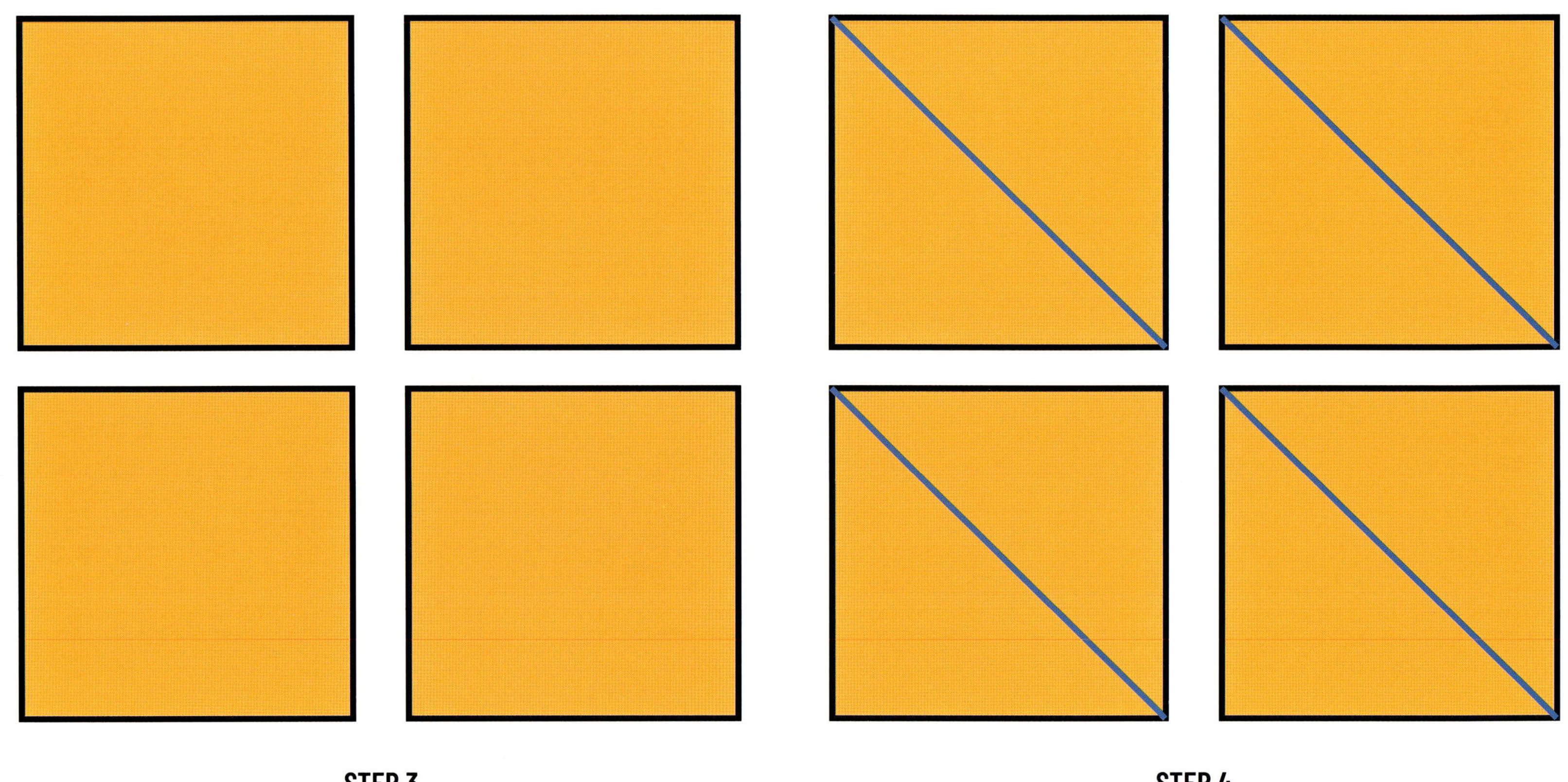

STEP 3 **STEP 4**

5. Place a 5" x 5" (12.7 x 12.7cm) square right sides together with a 10" x 10" (25.4 x 25.4cm) square. Position it so the corners line up as shown and the drawn line cuts through the corner of the 10" x 10" (25.4 x 25.4cm) square.

6. Stitch on the drawn line.

7. Cut ¼" (6.4mm) away from the drawn line as shown.

8. Repeat with the opposite corner of the 10" (25.4cm) square.

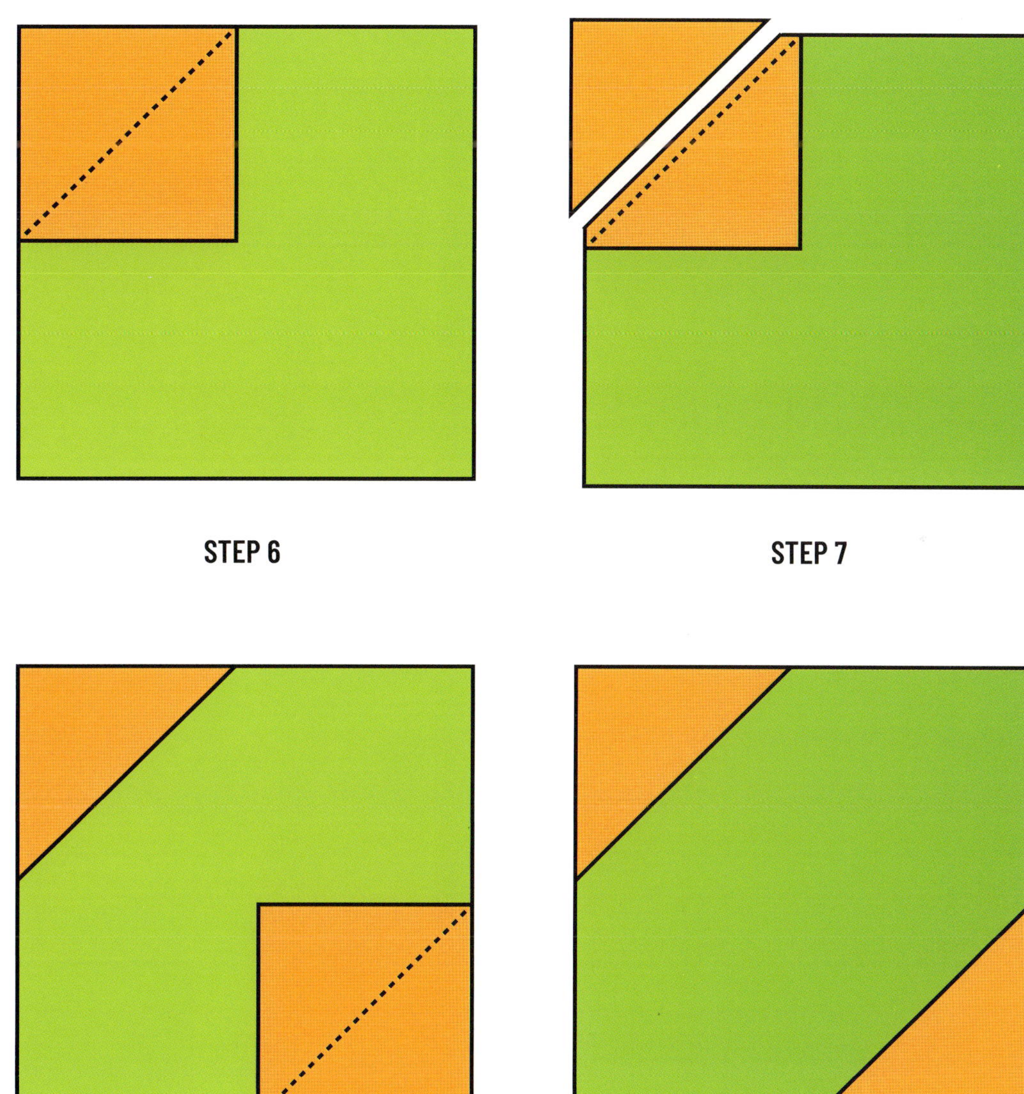

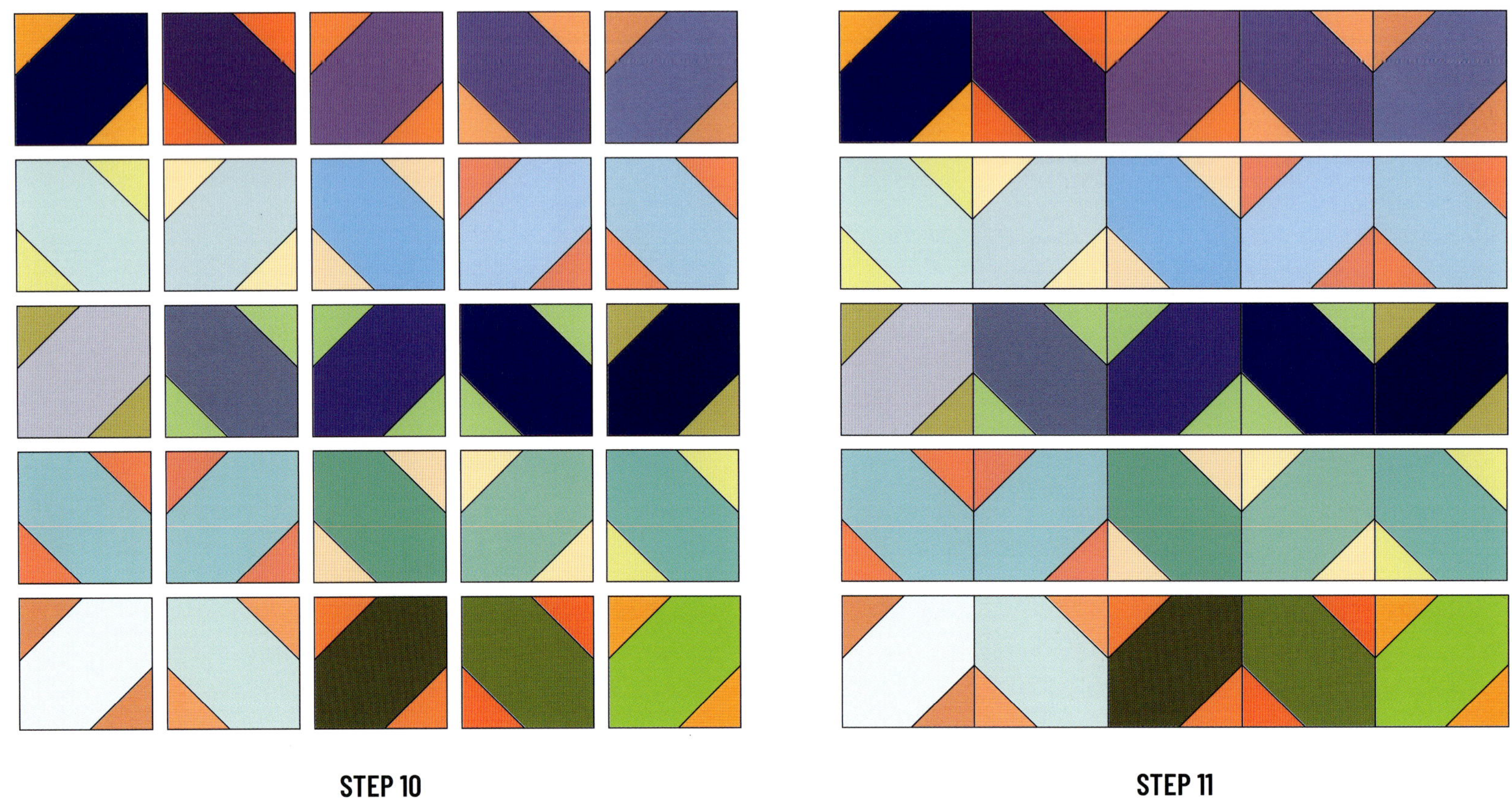

9. Repeat on all (25) 10" (25.4cm) squares.

10. Lay out the blocks into five rows of five blocks each. See the diagrams on pages 52–53 for examples.

11. Stitch the blocks into rows. Press the seams in alternating directions.

STEP 12

12. Stitch the rows together. Press the seams in one direction.

13. Add borders if desired. See the section on adding borders on page 115.

14. Quilt and bind as desired. See the sections on quilting and binding starting on page 117 for more ideas.

Layout Options

Each layout offers a different take on the quilt design. Follow one exactly, or let it guide your improvisation.

LAYOUT OPTION 1: HUGS AND KISSES

LAYOUT OPTION 2: TILTED TILES

LAYOUT OPTION 3: POINTED PATH

LAYOUT OPTION 4: DIAMOND NEST

Rail Fence

Though the Rail Fence is a classic quilt design, the straight lines give it a wonderful modern look when used with modern fabrics. The blocks are simple to piece with lots of straight stitching.

Squared-Up Block Size: 8½" (21.6cm)
Finished Block Size: 8" (20.3cm)
Finished Quilt Size: 48" x 56" (122 x 142.2cm)

Tools:

Quilting Rulers • Rotary Cutter
Cutting Mat • Iron and Ironing Board
Sewing Machine • Thread • Batting

Materials:

(42) 10" (25.4cm) squares

Instructions:

For these variations, you may need to make one, two, or three of these blocks:

Block 1:

1. Square up the 10" (25.4cm) square to 8½" x 8½" (21.6 x 21.6cm).

Block 2:

1. Cut 1½" (3.81cm) off the bottom of the 10" (25.4cm) square.

2. This will leave a 10" x 8½" (25.4 x 21.6cm) rectangle. Cut into four 2½" x 8½" (6.4 x 21.6cm) strips.

3. Shuffle the strips. Sew sets of four together to make the block. Press the seams in one direction. This block will square up to 8½" x 8½" (21.6 x 21.6cm).

STEP 1

STEP 2

Block 3:

1. Cut a 10" (25.4cm) square into four 2½" x 10" (6.4 x 25.4cm) strips.

2. Subcut each of these strips into four 2½" (6.4cm) squares for a total of 16 squares.

3. Shuffle these squares and lay them out randomly or in a pattern.

4. Stitch the squares into rows. Press the seams in each row in alternating directions.

5. Stitch the rows together. Press the seams in one direction.

STEP 1

STEP 2

STEP 3

STEP 4

STEP 5

Layout Options

For the different layouts, you'll need to make a different number of the different styles of blocks. Refer to the chart below. For each block, you'll need one of the 10" squares. (For example, if you need 12 blocks, you'll use 12 of the 10" squares.)

For Layout 1:

1. Select 12 squares to make 12 of Block 1.

2. Select 21 squares to make 21 of Block 2.

3. Select nine squares to make nine of Block 3.

4. Make the units as described on pages 56 and 57. Lay out the units. Sew into rows. Press the seams in each row in alternating directions.

5. Stitch the rows together. Press the seams in one direction.

	Layout 1	Layout 2
Block 1	12	21
Block 2	21	21
Block 3	9	0

STEP 4

LAYOUT OPTION 1: CORNER PATCH

For Layout 2:

1. Select 21 squares to make 21 of Block 1.

2. Select 21 squares to make 21 of Block 2.

3. Make the units as described on pages 56 and 57. Lay out the units. Sew into rows. Press the seams in each row in alternating directions.

4. Stitch the rows together. Press the seams in one direction.

LAYOUT OPTION 2: MODERN RAILS

Half Rail Fence

A fun twist on the traditional Rail Fence quilt block, the Half Rail Fence provides even more variety. Great for using fun colors and prints, the seams going in multiple directions add a lot of dimension to this quilt block. This quilt works great without needing to divide the squares by color or value.

Squared-Up Block Size: 8½" (21.6cm)
Finished Block Size: 8" (20.3cm)
Finished Quilt Size: 48" x 56" (122 x 142.2cm)

Tools:

Quilting Rulers • Rotary Cutter
Cutting Mat • Iron and Ironing Board
Sewing Machine • Thread • Batting

Materials:

(42) 10" (25.4cm) squares

Instructions:

1. Carefully cut all the 10" (25.4cm) squares as shown in the diagram. If you are experienced with rotary cutting, you can cut the squares in stacks of three to five at a time. The most accurate way is to cut the square into three strips: ½" (1.3cm), 4½" (11.4cm), and 5" (12.7cm). The ½" (1.3cm) strip can be discarded.

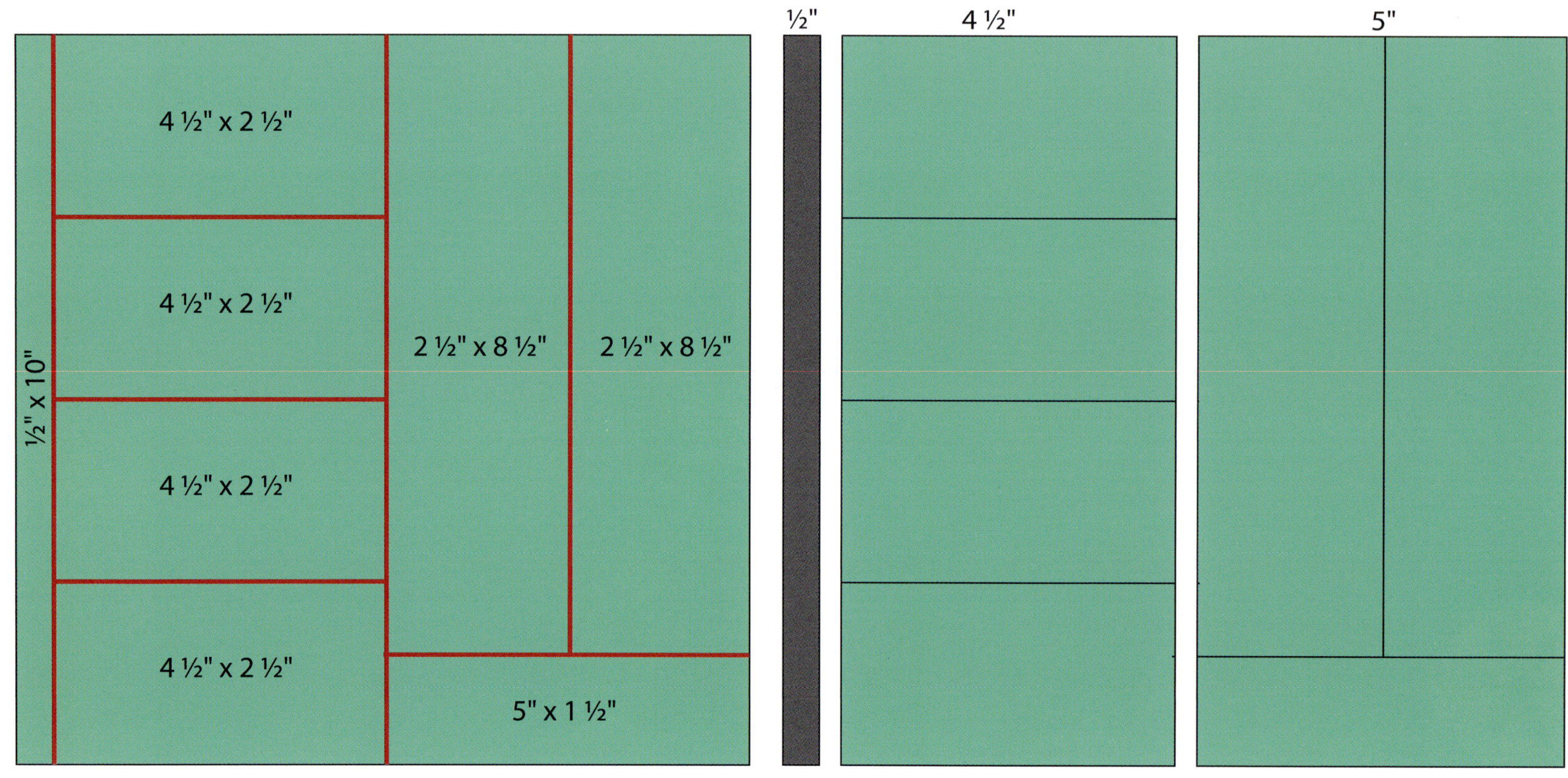

STEP 1

STEP 2

STEP 3

2. Now cut the 4½" (11.4cm) strip into four 4½" x 2½" (11.4 x 6.4cm) rectangles. Trim 1½" (3.8cm) off the bottom of the 5" (12.7cm) strip. This 1½" x 5" (3.8 x 12.7cm) piece can be discarded.

3. Cut the 5" x 8½" (12.7 x 21.6cm) strip in half to make two 2½" x 8½" (6.4 x 21.6cm) strips. This completes the cutting.

4. Shuffle the fabrics. Sew four 4½" x 2½" (11.4 x 6.4cm) rectangles as shown. Press the seams in one direction.

5. Sew two 2½" x 8½" (6.4 x 21.6cm) rectangles as shown. Press the seams in one direction.

6. Stitch together the units from steps 4 and 5 as shown. Press the seams toward the 8½" (21.6cm) strips.

7. Lay out the units however you like—there are lots of options. Stitch into rows. Press the seams in each row in alternating directions.

8. Stitch the rows together. Press the seams in one direction.

9. Quilt and bind as desired. See the sections on quilting and binding starting on page 117 for more ideas.

Layout Options

Each layout offers a different take on the quilt design. Follow one exactly, or let it guide your improvisation.

LAYOUT OPTION 1: TWIST AND TURN

LAYOUT OPTION 2: WOVEN WHIMSY

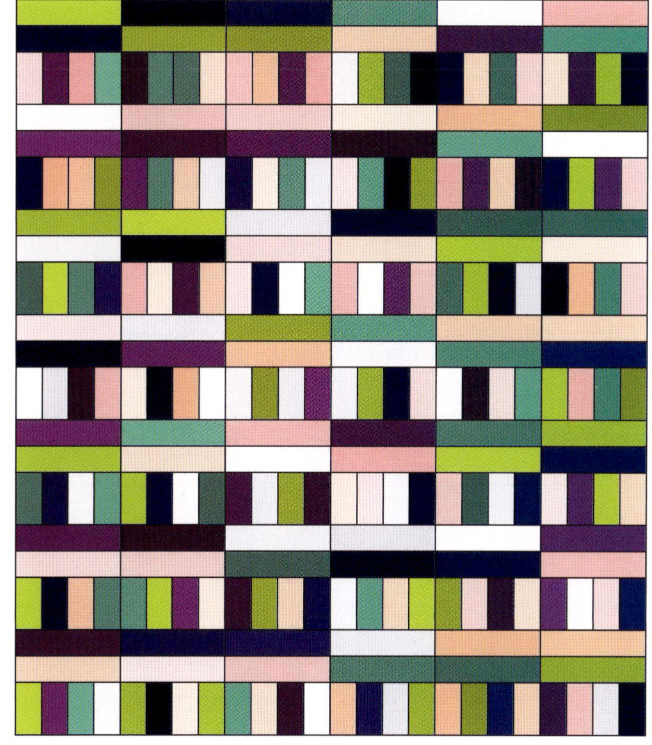

LAYOUT OPTION 3: RAIL RHYTHM

LAYOUT OPTION 4: PATCH PULSE

LAYOUT OPTION 5: COLOR CASCADE

LAYOUT OPTION 6: GRIDLOCK

An alternate layout for this quilt.

Half-Quarter-Square Triangles

Play with color and movement using the Half-Quarter-Square Triangle blocks in this quilt! Great for fabric collections with both large and small prints, you'll love laying out the finished blocks to make unique designs.

Squared-Up Block Size: 9" (22.9cm)
Finished Block Size: 8½" (21.6cm)
Finished Quilt Size: 51" x 51" (130 x 130cm)

Tools:

Quilting Rulers • Rotary Cutter
Cutting Mat • Iron and Ironing Board • Marking Pens
Sewing Machine • Thread • Batting

Materials:

(42) 10" (25.4cm) squares

Instructions:

1. Divide your forty-two 10" (25.4cm) squares into three piles. One will have 18 squares (Pile 1), and the other two will have 9 squares each (Piles 2 and 3). You'll have six squares left over.

2. Draw a diagonal line on the back of each of the squares in Pile 2.

3. Pair each square in Pile 1 with a square in Pile 2. Place them right sides together and stitch ¼" (6.4mm) away from each side of the drawn line.

4. Cut on the drawn line. Open each half and press toward the dark color.

5. Draw a diagonal line on the back of each of the squares in Pile 3. Place each right sides together with the half-square triangles made in step 4. The diagonal line should go in the opposite direction of the seam, so that they cross to make an X. The square from Pile 3 will be larger than the half-square triangle; this is okay.

6. Stitch ¼" (6.4mm) away from each side of the drawn line.

7. Cut on the line, open, and press toward the half-square triangle side (not the quarter-square triangles).

8. This will make 36 half-quarter-square triangle units.

9. Lay out your units in the desired configuration. See the diagrams on pages 73–75 for examples.

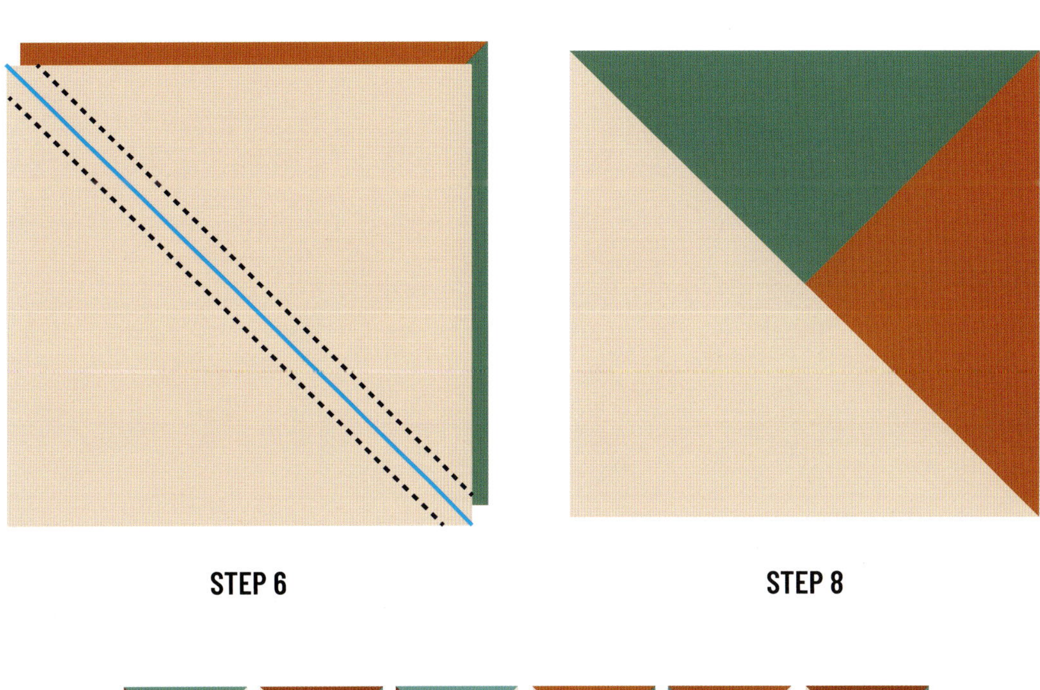

STEP 6 **STEP 8**

STEP 9

STEP 10

STEP 11

10. Stitch the blocks into rows. Press the seams in alternating directions.

11. Stitch the rows together. Press the seams in one direction.

12. Quilt and bind as desired. See the sections on quilting and binding starting on page 117 for more ideas.

Layout Options

Each layout offers a different take on the quilt design. Follow one exactly, or let it guide your improvisation.

LAYOUT OPTION 1: PRISM PATH

LAYOUT OPTION 2: TRIANGLE TIDE

LAYOUT OPTION 3: DIAGONAL HARMONY

LAYOUT OPTION 4: TWISTED ANGLES

LAYOUT OPTION 5: MIRROR MAZE

Square-in-a-Square

Perfect for fabrics with gradation throughout the fabric collection, the Square-in-a-Square block sews up quickly with simple, straight lines. By turning the blocks and offsetting the seams, you'll find that the blocks sew together quickly and easily to make the finished quilt top. This pattern can work great with any fabric collection, but it works especially well with high-contrast fabrics.

Squared-Up Block Size: 9" (22.9cm)
Finished Block Size: 8½" (21.6cm)
Finished Quilt Size: 51" x 51" (130 x 130cm)
or 51" x 59.5" (130 x 151.1cm)

Tools:

Quilting Rulers • Rotary Cutter
Cutting Mat • Iron and Ironing Board
Sewing Machine • Thread • Batting

Materials:

(42) 10" (25.4cm) squares

Instructions:

1. Place the fabrics in order from darkest to lightest, 1–42.

2. Cut two 2½" (6.4cm) strips off the top and bottom.

3. Trim the top and bottom strips to 2½" x 9" (6.4 x 22.9cm).

4. From the center 5" (12.7cm) strip, cut into three parts: a 2½" x 5" (6.4 x 12.7cm) piece, a 5" x 5" (12.7 x 12.7cm) piece, and a second 2½" x 5" (6.4 x 12.7cm) piece.

5. Shuffle the center fabrics so that each square has a center that does not match the borders. You will keep all four border pieces the same, only swapping out the centers. For maximum contrast, swap so that each light border has a dark center, and each dark border has a light center.

6. Stitch the 2½" x 5" (6.4 x 12.7cm) strip to one side of the 5" (12.7cm) center square. Press the seam out.

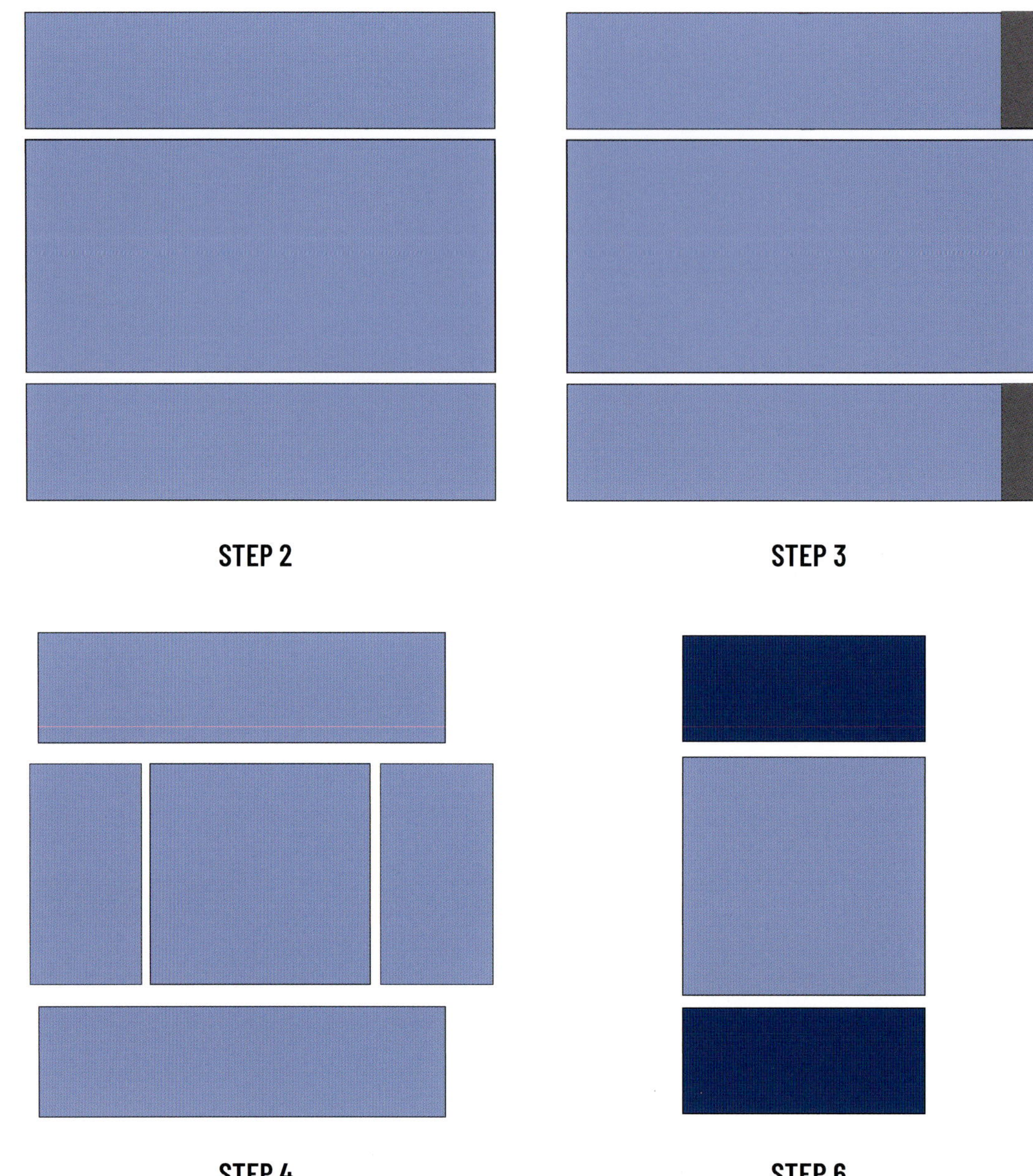

7. Stitch the remaining 2½" x 5" (6.4 x 12.7cm) strip to the other side of the 5" (12.7cm) center square. Press the seam out.

8. This makes your block. Make a total of 42 blocks.

9. Lay out your units in the desired configuration. Alternate the directions of the seams on the top and the sides to reduce the bulk from the seams.

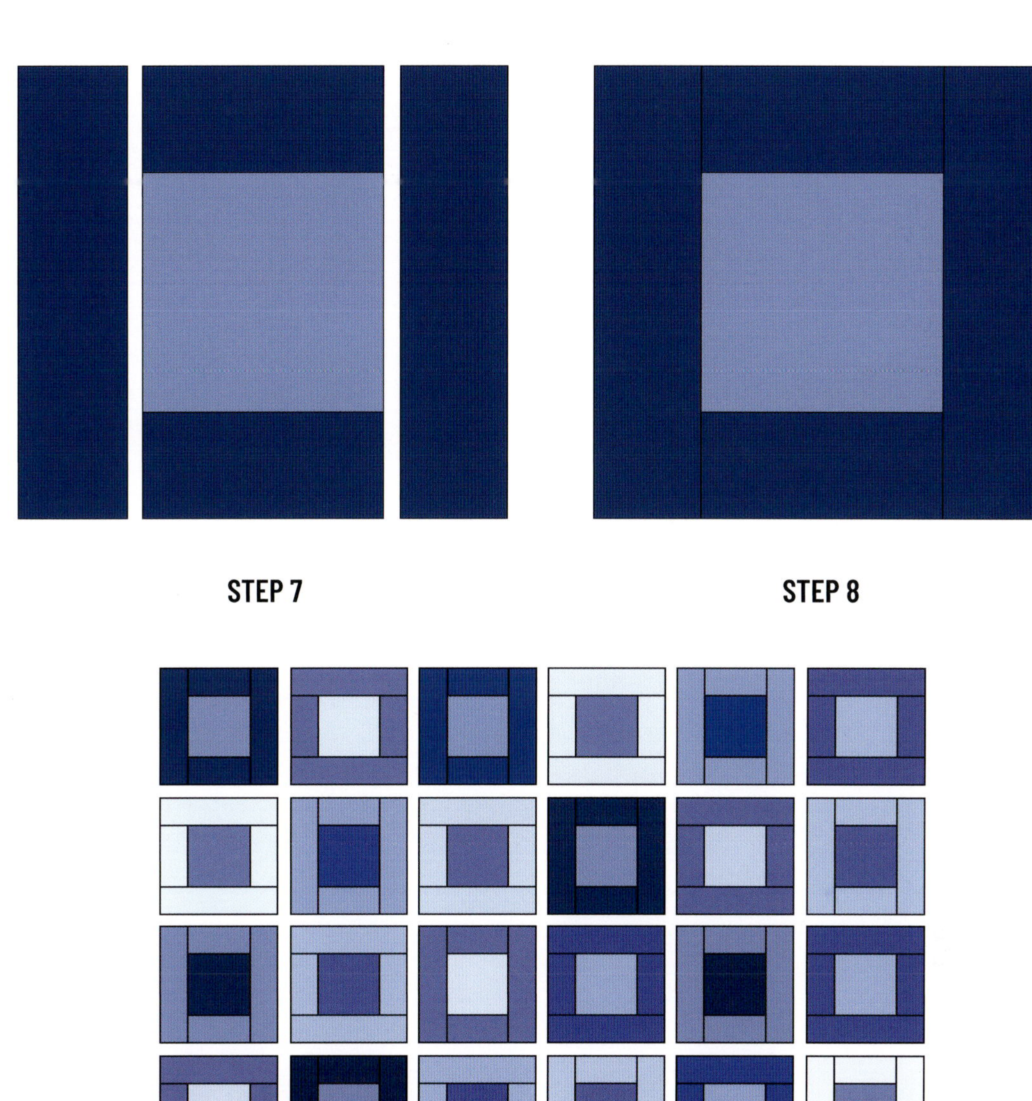

STEP 7

STEP 8

STEP 9

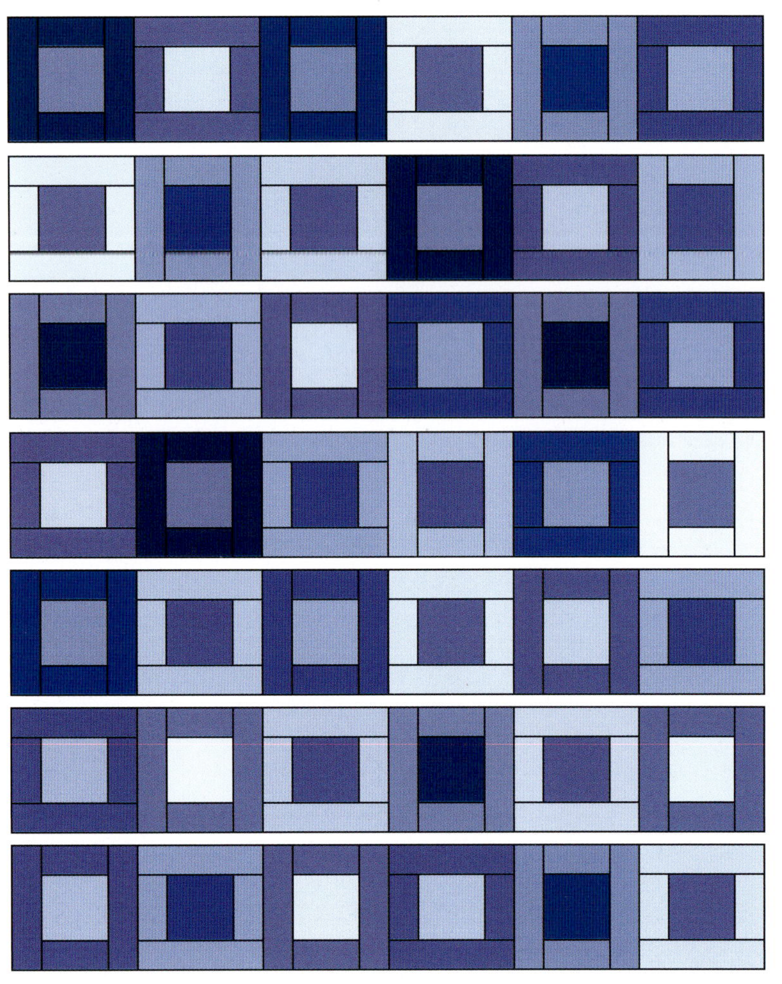

STEP 10

STEP 11

10. Stitch the blocks into rows. Press the seams in alternating directions.

11. Stitch the rows together. Press the seams in one direction.

12. Quilt and bind as desired. See the sections on quilting and binding starting on page 117 for more ideas.

Layout Options

Each layout offers a different take on the quilt design. Follow one exactly, or let it guide your improvisation.

LAYOUT OPTION 1: STACKED SQUARES

LAYOUT OPTION 2: BOXED IN

Nine-Patch

If you love a scrappy-yet-cohesive-looking quilt, the Nine-Patch is exactly what you're looking for! These blocks come together quickly and have the traditional scrappy flair of a nine-patch. Alternate with uncut blocks for a quilt that is just as scrappy, with half the sewing needed. This pattern can work great with any fabric collection, but it's especially impressive with high-contrast fabrics. For the different layouts, you'll need to make a different number of the different styles of blocks. Refer to the chart below. For each block, you'll need one of the 10" squares. (For example, if you need 12 blocks, you'll use 12 of the 10" squares.)

Squared-Up Block Size: 8½" (21.6cm)
Finished Block Size: 8" (20.3cm)
Finished Quilt Size: 48" x 56" (122 x 142.2cm)

Tools:

Quilting Rulers • Rotary Cutter
Cutting Mat • Iron and Ironing Board
Sewing Machine • Thread • Batting

Materials:

(42) 10" (25.4cm) squares

	Layout 1	Layout 2
Block 1	21	0
Block 2	21	42

Instructions:

Block 1:

1. Square up the units to 8" x 8" (20.3 x 20.3cm). Set aside.

Block 2:

1. Cut the squares into three 3" (7.6cm) strips. You'll be trimming off 1" (2.5cm).

2. Subcut each of the strips into three 3" x 3" (7.6 x 7.6cm) squares. You'll be trimming off 1" (2.5cm).

3. Shuffle the fabrics. Use two fabrics for each block as shown.

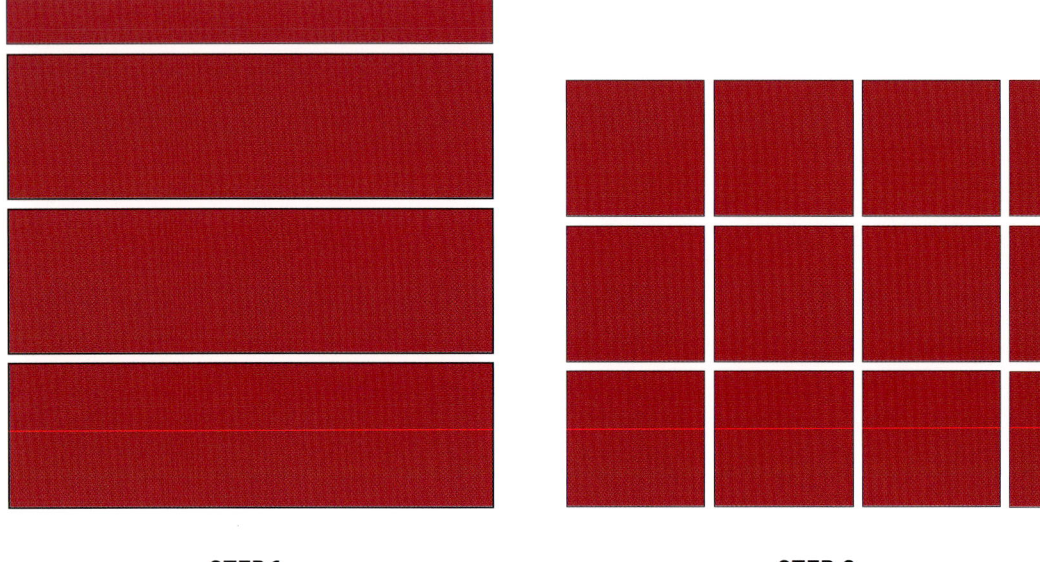

STEP 1

STEP 2

STEP 3

4. Stitch into rows. Press the seams in each row in opposite directions.

5. Stitch the rows together. Press the seams in one direction.

6. This makes your block. Make a total of 42 blocks.

7. Lay out your units in the desired configuration. See page 87 for layout options.

STEP 4

STEP 5

STEP 7

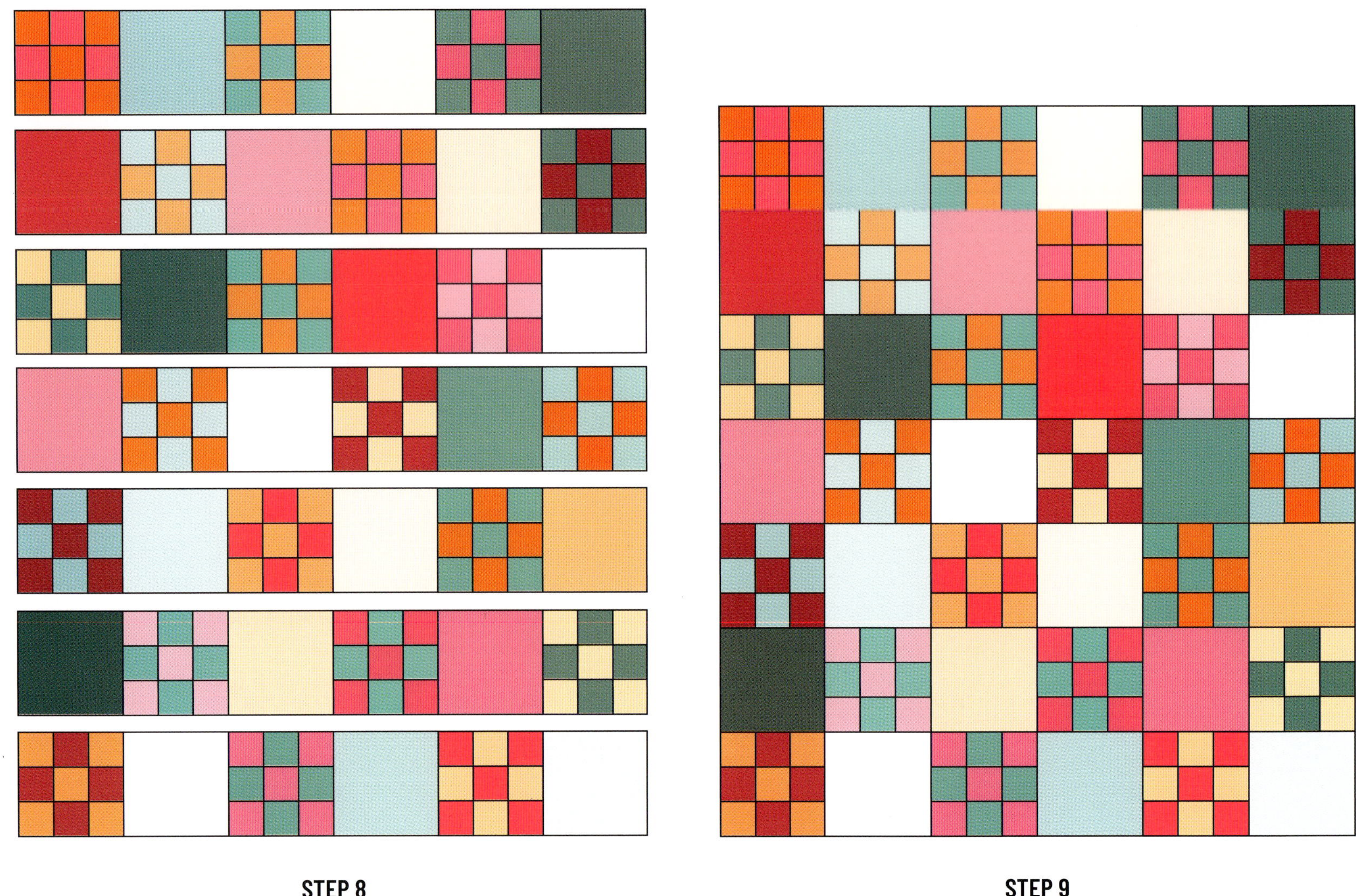

STEP 8

STEP 9

8. Stitch the blocks into rows. Press the seams in alternating directions.

9. Stitch the rows together. Press the seams in one direction.

10. Quilt and bind as desired. See the sections on quilting and binding starting on page 117 for more ideas.

Layout Options

Each layout offers a different take on the quilt design. Follow one exactly, or let it guide your improvisation.

LAYOUT OPTION 1: BLOCK BREAK

LAYOUT OPTION 2: PATCH PARTY

Quarter-Square Triangles

These hourglass-style Quarter-Square Triangle quilt blocks help provide a cohesive look to a scrappy quilt. Play with the rotation of the blocks or add in uncut blocks to get a completely different-looking quilt.

Squared-Up Block Size: 9" (22.9cm)
Finished Block Size: 8½" (21.6cm)
Finished Quilt Size: 51" x 59.5" (130 x 151.1cm)

Tools:

Quilting Rulers • Rotary Cutter • Cutting Mat
Marking Pens • Iron and Ironing Board
Sewing Machine • Thread • Batting

Materials:

(42) 10" (25.4cm) squares

Instructions:

1. Divide your forty-two 10" (25.4cm) squares into two piles. Pile 1 will have the lighter squares, and Pile 2 will have the darker squares. Each pile will have 21 squares.

2. Draw a diagonal line on the back of each of the squares in Pile 1.

3. Pair each square in Pile 1 with a square in Pile 2. Place them right sides together and stitch ¼" (6.4mm) away from each side of the drawn line.

4. Cut on the drawn line. Open each half and press toward the dark color.

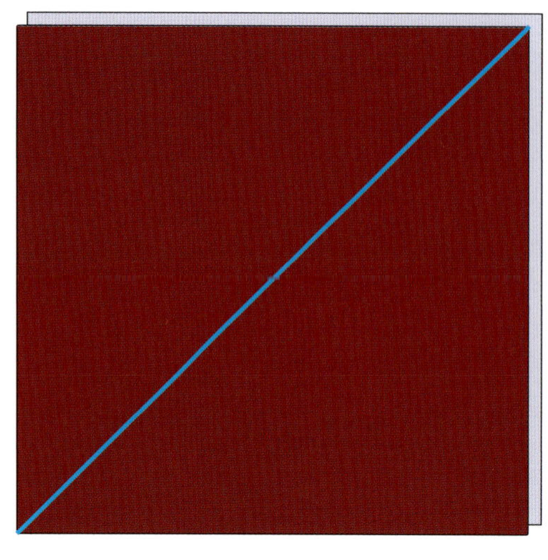

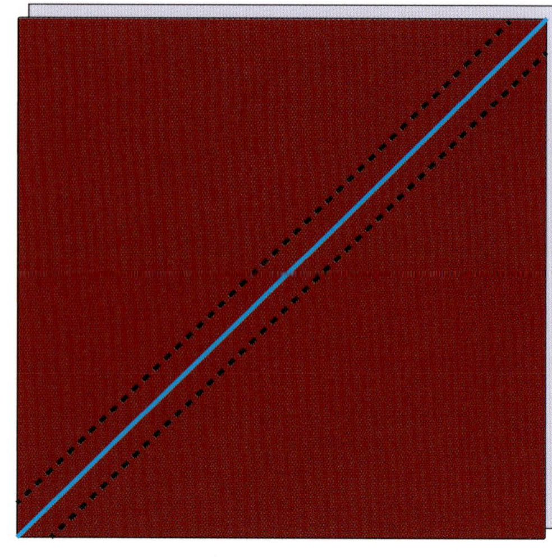

STEP 4

5. Place two half-square triangles right sides together, with the seams lined up. The alternate fabrics should be touching one another. Draw a diagonal line in the opposite direction of the seam as shown.

6. Stitch ¼" (6.4mm) away from each side of the drawn line.

7. Cut on the line, open, and spin the seams or press in one direction. This is your quarter-square triangle unit. This will make 42 units.

8. Lay out your units in the desired configuration. See the diagrams on page 93 for examples.

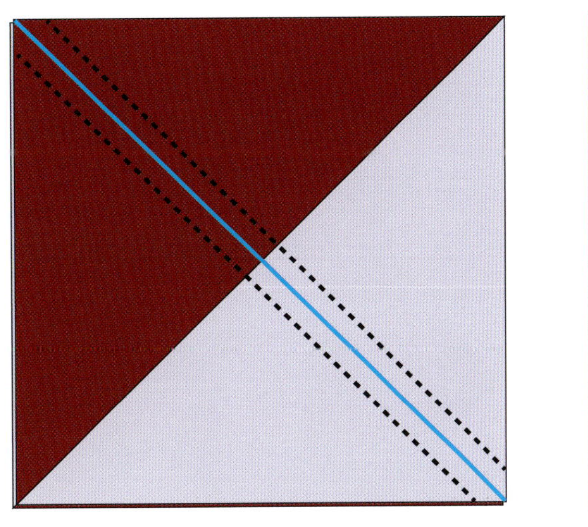

STEP 6

STEP 7

STEP 8

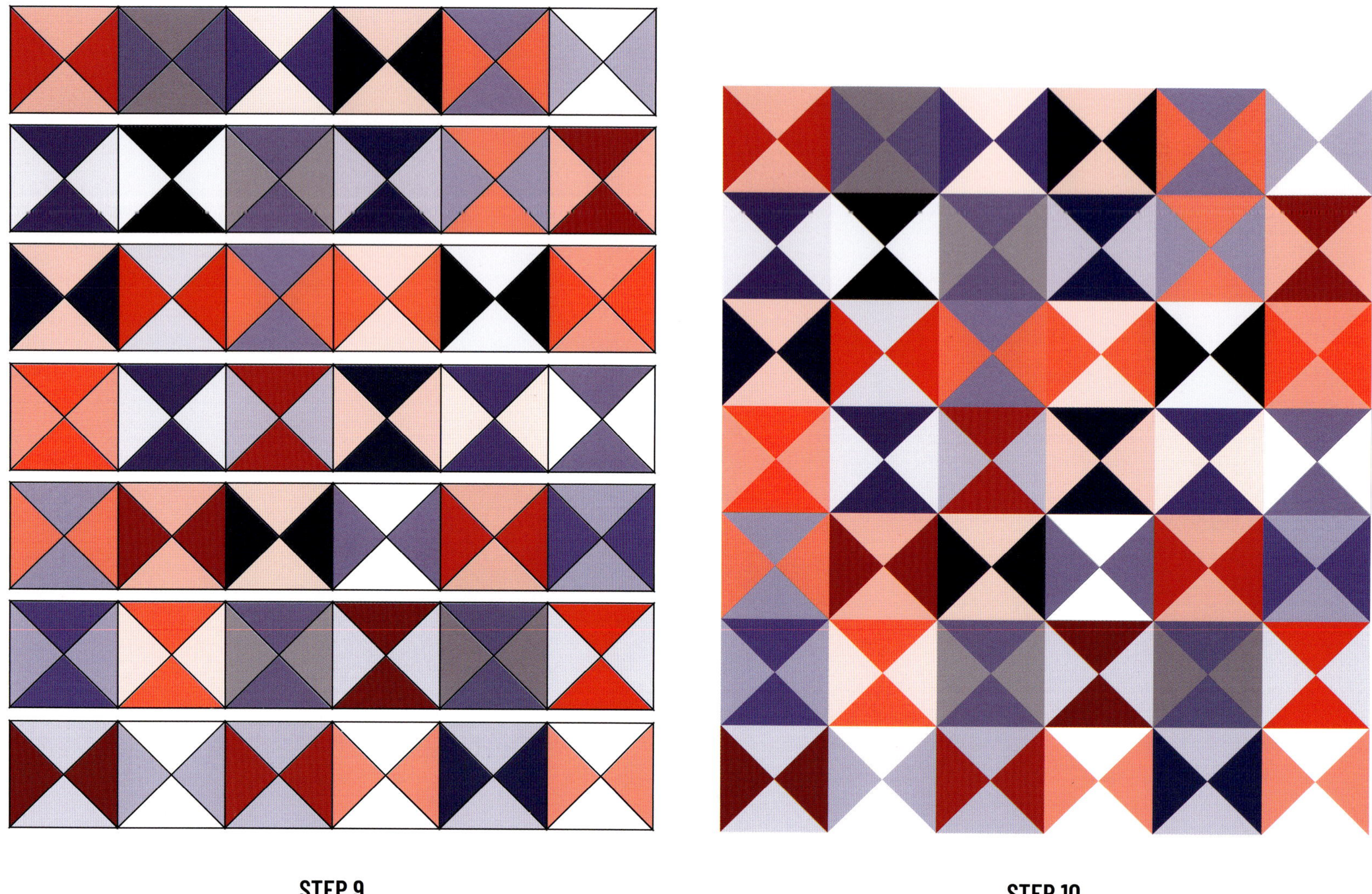

STEP 9

STEP 10

9. Stitch the blocks into rows. Press the seams in alternating directions.

10. Stitch the rows together. Press the seams in one direction.

11. Quilt and bind as desired. See the sections on quilting and binding starting on page 117 for more ideas.

Layout Options

Each layout offers a different take on the quilt design. Follow one exactly, or let it guide your improvisation.

LAYOUT OPTION 2: TIED TOGETHER

LAYOUT OPTION 1: HOURGLASS TWIST

LAYOUT OPTION 3: PATCH BOW

Quarter Log Cabin

With this simpler version of the traditional Log Cabin block, you can combine multiple Quarter Log Cabins to create a "faux" Log Cabin look, or you can lay out the blocks to make original designs. It's a quick make that works with nearly any fabric collection.

Squared-Up Block Size: 8½" (21.6cm)
Finished Block Size: 8" (20.3cm)
Finished Quilt Size: 48" x 56" (122 x 142.2cm)

Tools:

Quilting Rulers • Rotary Cutter
Cutting Mat • Iron and Ironing Board
Sewing Machine • Thread • Batting

Materials:

(42) 10" (25.4cm) squares

Instructions:

1. Cut all your pieces from the 10" (25.4cm) square as shown in the diagram.

2. From the bottom, trim off a 1" (2.5cm) strip, then a 3" (7.6cm) strip. Discard the 1" (2.5cm) strip. Trim the 3" (7.6cm) strip to 3" x 8" (7.6 x 20.3cm).

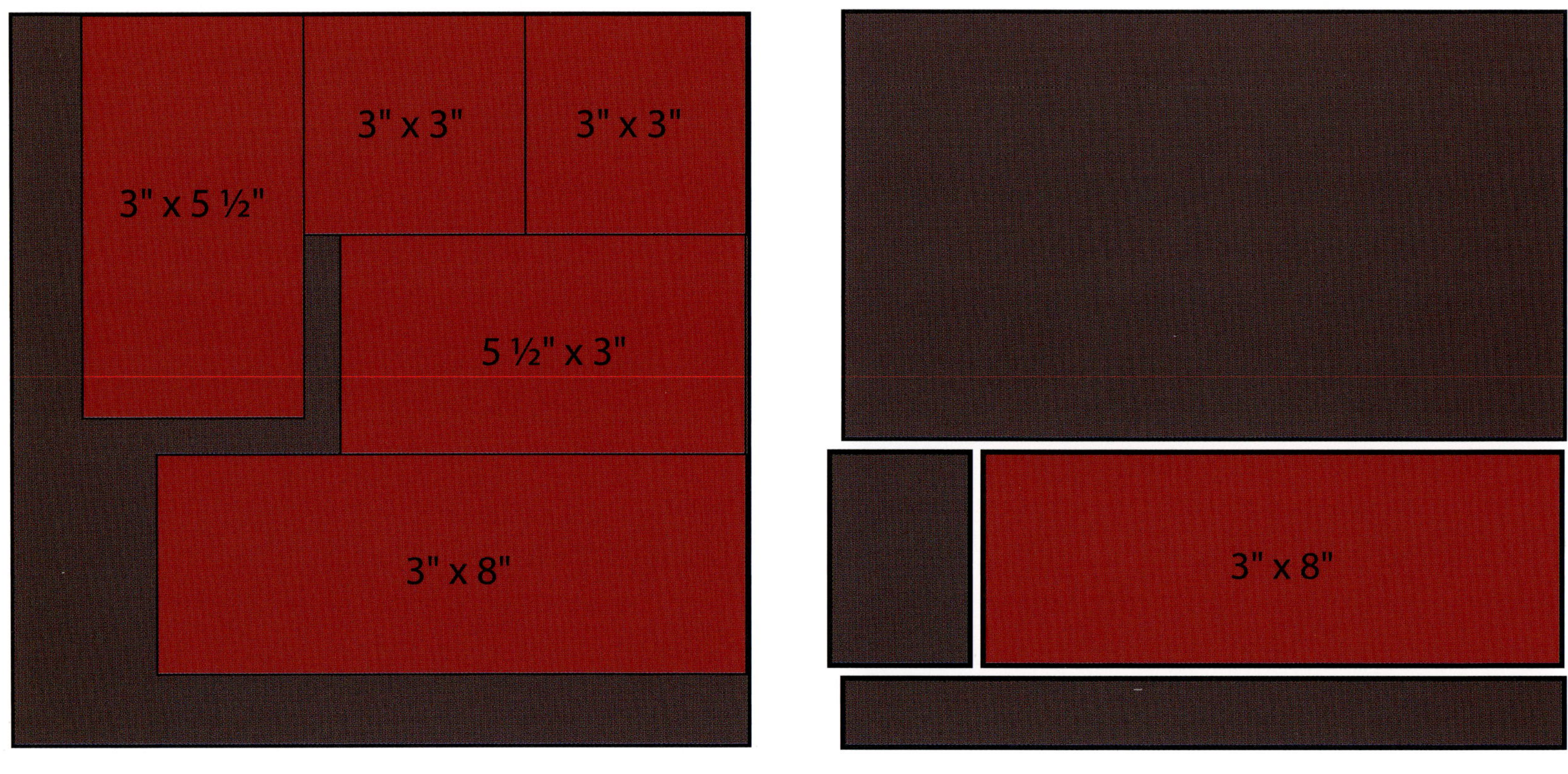

STEP 1

STEP 2

3. From the remaining strip, trim a 1" (2.5cm) strip, then cut a 3" (7.6cm) strip. Discard the 1" (2.5cm) strip. Trim the 3" (7.6cm) strip to 3" x 5½" (7.6 x 14cm).

4. Cut the remaining 6" x 6" (15.2 x 15.2cm) square in half to make two 3" x 6" (7.6 x 15.2cm) rectangles. Trim ½" (1.3cm) from one to make it 5½" x 3" (14 x 7.6cm).

5. Finally, cut the remaining 3" x 6" (7.6 x 15.2cm) piece in half to make two 3" x 3" (7.6 x 7.6cm) squares.

6. Shuffle the fabrics so that three different fabrics are used in the block as shown.

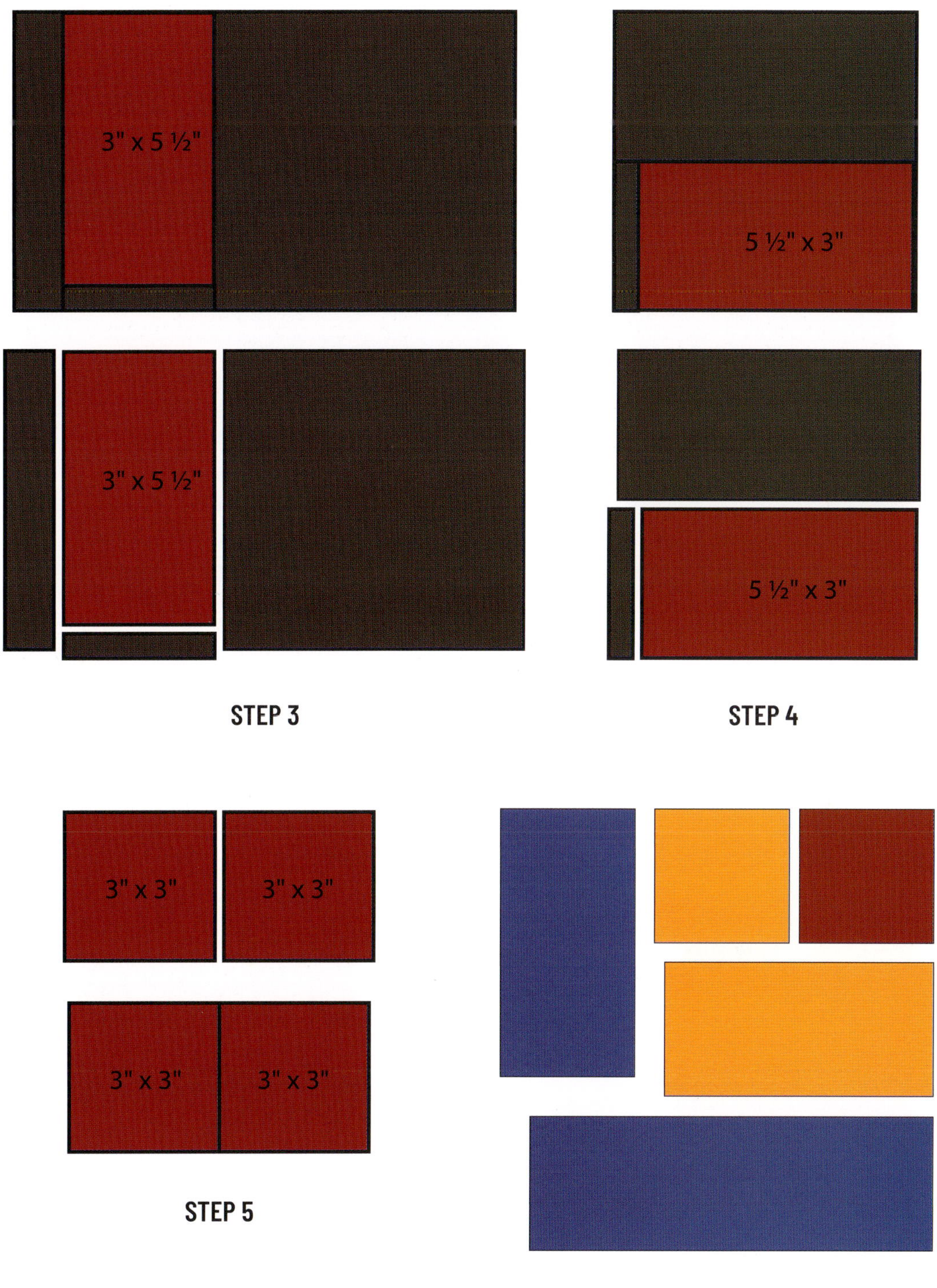

7. Stitch the 3" (7.6cm) squares together. Press the seams in one direction.

8. Stitch on the 5½" x 3" (14 x 7.6cm) as shown. Press toward this rectangle.

9. Stitch on the second 5½" x 3" (14 x 7.6cm) as shown. Press toward this rectangle.

10. Stitch on the 3" x 8" (7.6 x 20.3cm) rectangle as shown. Press toward this rectangle.

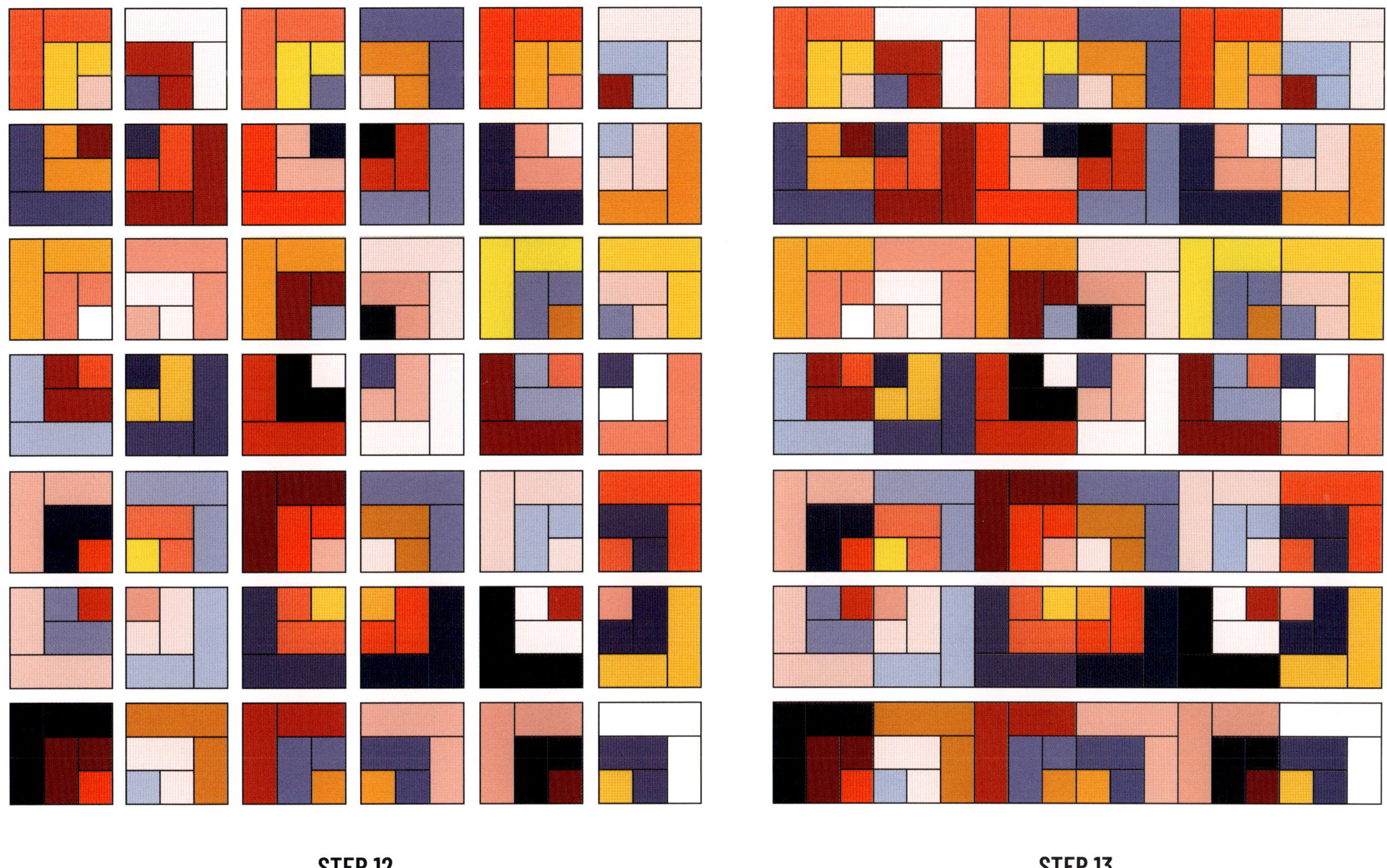

STEP 12

STEP 13

11. This makes your block. Make a total of 42 blocks.

12. Lay out your units in the desired configuration. See pages 101 to 103 for layout options.

13. Stitch the blocks into rows. Press the seams in each row in alternating directions.

STEP 14

14. Stitch the rows together. Press the seams in one direction.

15. Quilt and bind as desired. See the sections on quilting and binding starting on page 117 for more ideas.

Layout Options

Each layout offers a different take on the quilt design. Follow one exactly, or let it guide your improvisation.

LAYOUT OPTION 1: FRAMED QUARTERS

LAYOUT OPTION 2: CORNERSTONE

LAYOUT OPTION 3: CABIN COLUMNS

LAYOUT OPTION 4: LIGHTNING LOGS

An alternate layout for this quilt.

Specialty Designs

These fun designs work best with specific collections—or use a low-volume collection combined with leftover 10" (25.4cm) squares from other projects. These high-impact designs require very little cutting, so they come together very quickly.

Big Heart

This quilt was made by combining two different collections to have enough red fabrics for the heart, with contrasting low-volume fabrics for the background.

Squared-Up Block Size: 9½" (24.1cm)
Finished Block Size: 9" (22.9cm)
Finished Quilt Size: 54" x 54" (137.2 x 137.2cm) or 54" x 63"(137.2 x 160cm)

Tools:

Quilting Rulers • Rotary Cutter
Cutting Mat • Iron and Ironing Board
Sewing Machine • Thread • Batting

Materials:

(42) 10" (25.4cm) squares

Instructions:

1. Select five background and five red squares. Draw a diagonal line on the back of all the background squares.

2. Pair each of these 5 background squares with a red square. Place them right sides together and stitch ¼" (6.4mm) away from each side of the drawn line.

3. Cut on the drawn line. Open each half and press toward the dark color.

4. This will make 10 half-square triangle units.

5. Square up all squares and half-square triangles to 9" (22.9cm).

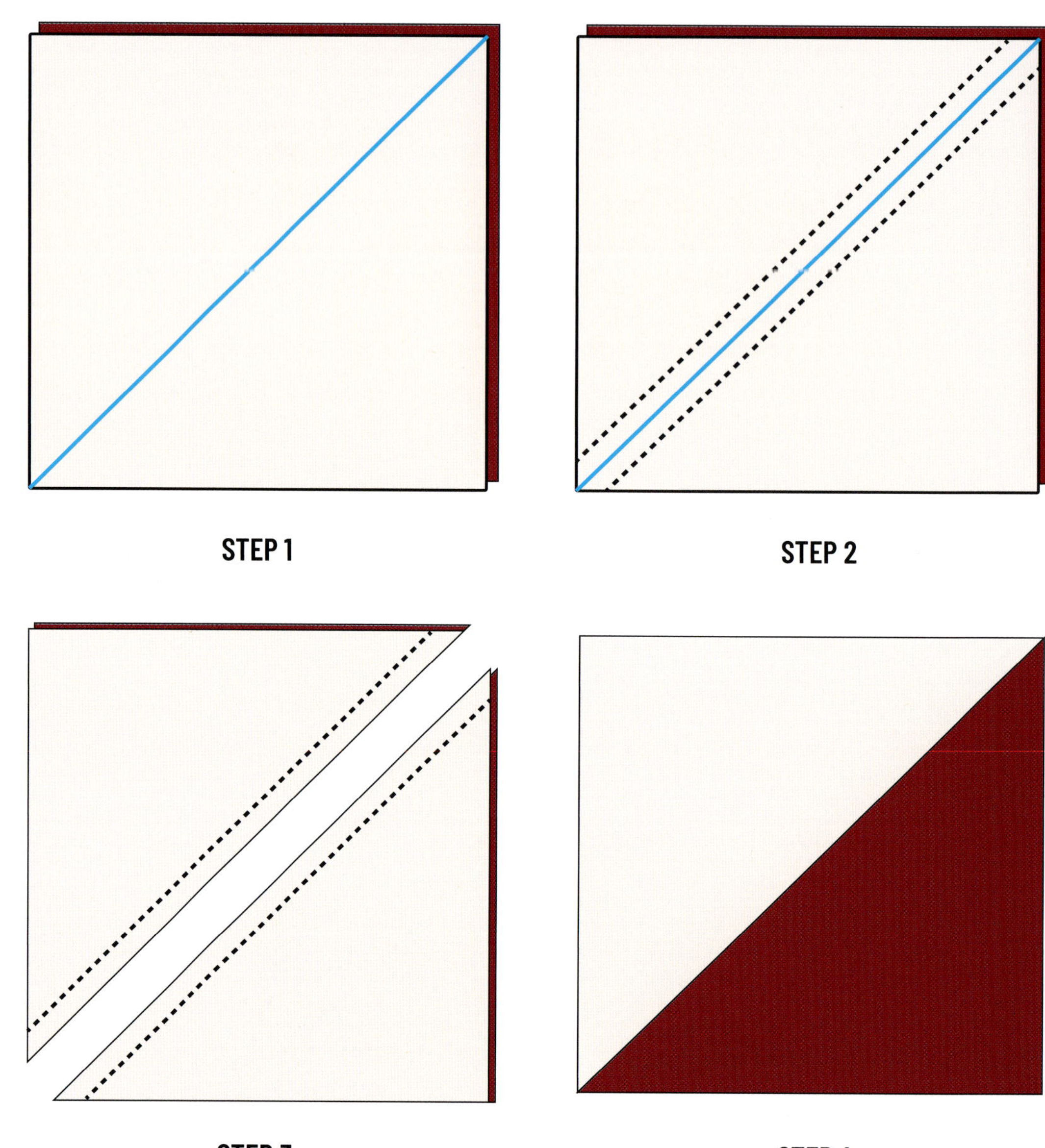

6. Lay out your units in the configuration as shown.

7. Stitch the blocks into rows. Press the seams in alternating directions.

8. Stitch the rows together. Press the seams in one direction.

9. Quilt and bind as desired. See the sections on quilting and binding starting on page 117 for more ideas.

STEP 6

STEP 7

STEP 8

Star

This quilt calls for a subtle contrast between the six star pieces and the remaining background squares.

Squared-Up Block Size: 9½" (24.1cm)
Finished Block Size: 9" (22.9cm)
Finished Quilt Size: 54" x 54" (137.2 x 137.2cm) or 54" x 63" (137.2 x 160cm)

Tools:

Quilting Rulers • Rotary Cutter
Cutting Mat • Iron and Ironing Board
Sewing Machine • Thread • Batting

Materials:

(42) 10" (25.4cm) squares

Instructions:

1. Draw a diagonal line on the back of six of the background squares.

2. Pair each of these six background squares with a star square. Place them right sides together and stitch ¼" (6.4mm) away from each side of the drawn line.

3. Cut on the drawn line. Open each half and press toward the dark color. This will make 12 half-square triangle units.

4. Square up all squares and half-square triangles to 9" (22.9cm).

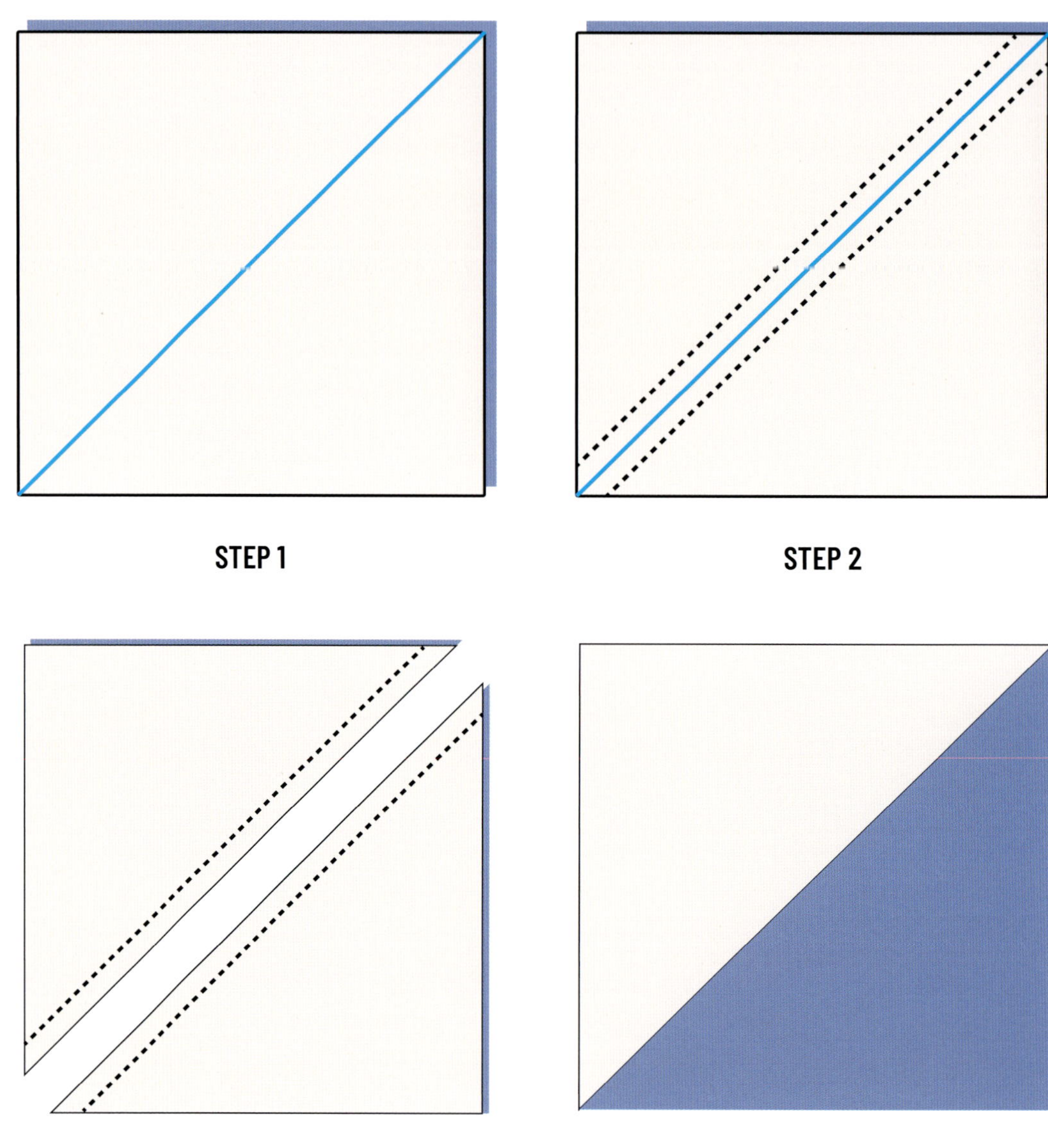

5. Lay out your units in the configuration as shown.

6. Stitch the blocks into rows. Press the seams in alternating directions.

7. Stitch the rows together. Press the seams in one direction.

8. Quilt and bind as desired. See the sections on quilting and binding starting on page 117 for more ideas.

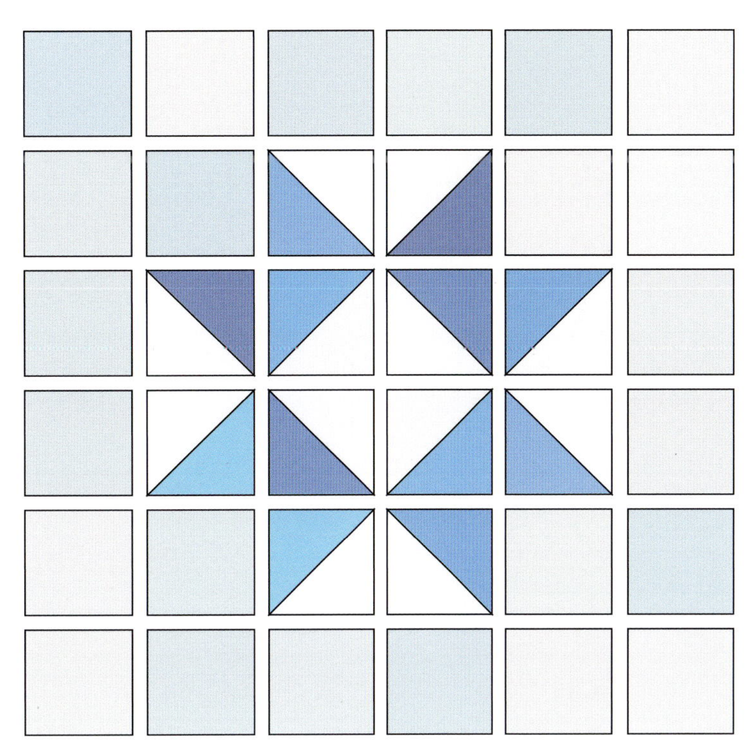

STEP 5

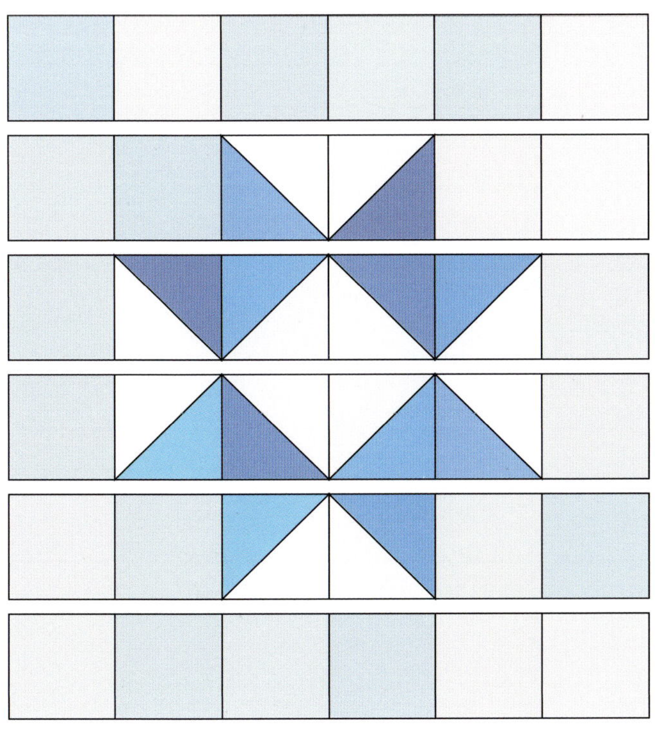

STEP 6

STEP 7

Adjusting Total Quilt Sizes

Making quilts larger or smaller is as easy as adding more fabric! When buying the fabric for your project, consider the purpose of the quilt. Most of the quilts in this book are designed to be lap-sized quilts or baby quilts. However, they can easily be made into bed-sized quilts by adding more fabric. You can purchase extra sets of 10" squares to make more quilt blocks. Buy sets of the same fabric line for a more cohesive look to your quilt. Another option is to add a border—or multiple borders—to your quilt to bring it up to bed size.

Standard Quilt Sizes

- Baby 30" x 40" (76.2 x 101.6cm)
- Throw 50" x 65" (127 x 165.1cm)
- Twin 70" x 90" (177.8cm x 228.6cm)
- Queen 90" x 108" (228.6 x 274.3cm)
- King 110" x 108" (279.4 x 274.3cm)

Adding More Blocks

For many of these designs, you can add more blocks to your quilt. To determine how many total blocks you will need, follow these steps:

1. Determine the finished size of the quilt by using the standard quilt sizes above.

2. Determine the finished size of the quilt blocks by locating it on the page of the pattern.

3. Divide the width of the quilt by the finished size of the block. Round up to a whole number of blocks. This will tell you the number of blocks in each row.

4. Divide the height of the quilt by the finished size of the block. Round up to a whole number of blocks. This will tell you the number of rows in the quilt.

5. Multiply the number of blocks in each row by the number of rows. This will tell you the number of blocks you will need to make to complete your quilt.

Make your quilt bigger by adding more blocks or by adding a border.

9" FINISHED SQUARES

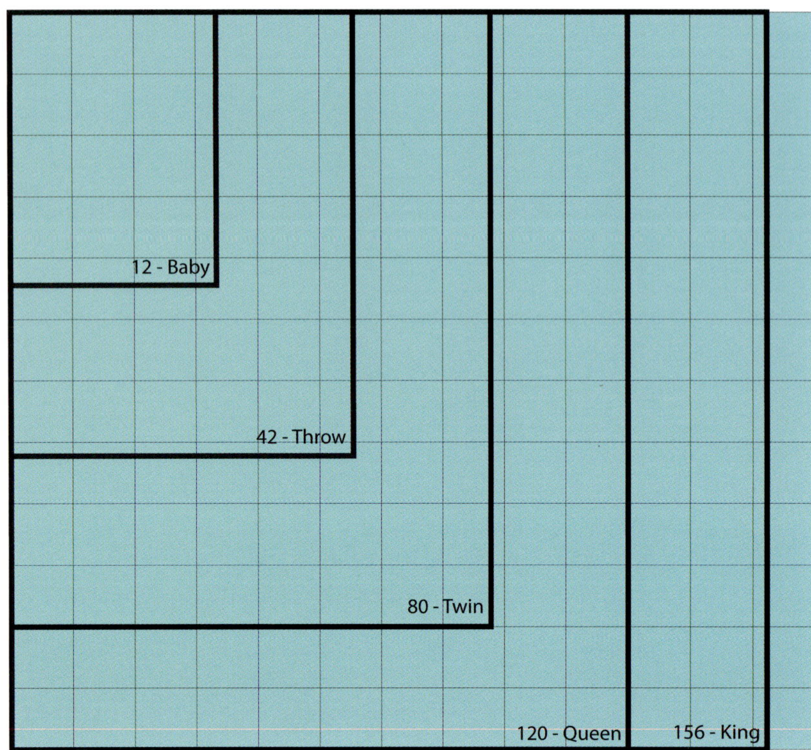

7½" FINISHED SQUARES

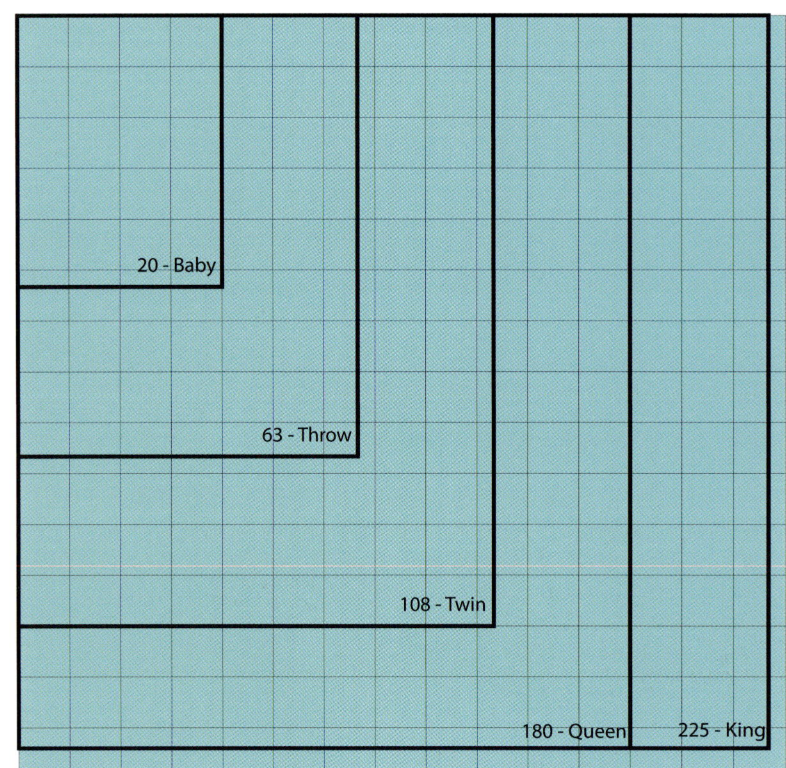

These grids provide a quick guide for how many 9" or 7½" finished squares you'll need for each of the standard quilt sizes. You can also see the sizes relative to each other on the grid.

Adding Borders

Rather than piecing more and more blocks to make a larger quilt, you can add borders to your quilt. This is often faster than piecing additional blocks. Many quilters prefer adding borders to bed-sized quilts since the center of the quilt is primarily on display, while the borders hang down the sides of the bed and are not always in view. Borders also add a beautiful frame to a quilt. Picking border fabrics that complement the colors in the quilt blocks can help to "bring forward" certain colors in the pieced blocks.

You can add one border or several borders. Traditionally, borders get larger as they move out from the center of a quilt. For example, the first border might be 2" (5.1cm), the second might be 4" (10.2cm), and the third could be 6" (15.2cm) or 8" (20.3cm). You can play with these sizes to create interest or drama.

To decide what size border(s) you need for your quilt, follow these steps:

1. Determine the desired finished size of the quilt by using the standard quilt sizes on page 112.

2. Determine the finished size of the quilt pattern by locating it on the page of the pattern.

3. Subtract the width of the quilt from the width of the desired finished quilt.

4. Subtract the height of the quilt pattern from the height of the desired finished quilt.

5. Select which is the larger of steps 3 and 4. The larger number is the number of inches that will be added by your border(s).

6. Divide the number in half. This is the number of inches that will be added to each side of the quilt by your border(s).

7. Based on this number, decide the number of borders you would like and how large they will be. For example, for 8" borders, you could choose a single 8" (20.3cm) border; a 2" (5.1cm) inner border and a 6" (15.2cm) outer border; or a 1" (2.5cm) first border, a 2" (5.1cm) second border, and a 5" (12.7cm) third border.

8. Once you've determined the width of the border(s), add ½" (1.3cm) to each of these numbers for the seam allowance. This is the size you will cut your strips.

There are calculations you can do to determine how much fabric you will need for each of your borders. This can get more complicated with multiple borders. If you don't mind having a little extra fabric (I have never met a quilter who does!), follow these steps for each border:

1. Add together the desired length and width of the finished quilt. Multiply this by 2. This tells you the perimeter of the quilt.

2. Divide the perimeter of the quilt by 40. This tells you the number of strips you will want to cut. Add 1 to this number so that you have enough fabric for at least one extra strip, just in case.

3. Multiply the number of strips by the width of the strip (including the seam allowance). This will tell you the total number of inches you will need of that border fabric.

4. Divide the number of inches by 36. This will tell you the total number of yards you will need. If your number ends in a decimal point, use these guidelines to determine how to round to the appropriate ¼ yard:

- Up to 0.25: ¼ yard (22.9cm)
- From 0.25 to 0.5: ½ yard (45.7cm)
- From 0.5 to 0.75: ¾ yard (68.6cm)
- From 0.75 and above: increase to 1 full yard (91.4cm)

For example: 2.157 would become 2¼ yards (2.1m), 3.258 would become 3½ yards (3.2m), 4.536 would become 4¾ yards (4.3m), and 3.89 would become 4 yards (3.7m).

5. This image shows 7½" (19cm) finished blocks, with 3" (7.6cm), 6" (15.2cm), and 9" (22.9cm) borders, bringing the quilt from smaller than twin to queen.

Finishing Your Quilt

There are many ways that you can finish your quilt. In this section, we'll go over how to traditionally finish your quilt. However, if you have another method for finishing your quilt that you prefer, you can do that. This is your quilt; you should be happy with the outcome!

"Quilting" the quilt is the process of securing the front, batting, and backing together using thread. A quilt can be quilted by hand, with hand stitches going through all the layers. Quilts can be quilted on a sewing machine as well. You may have access to a longarm quilting machine, or you can quilt it yourself on your domestic machine. If quilting it yourself feels daunting, you can choose to hire a longarm quilter to quilt it for you. Here is an overview of quilting your project yourself on your domestic sewing machine using a walking foot. This is the most accessible, and often easiest, method for quilting your project yourself.

Basting

1. Press your quilt top well, from both the back and the front. Make sure all the seams lay flat on the back. On the front, make sure the top lays smooth.

2. Cut your backing fabric. It should be at least 8" (20.3cm) taller and 8" (20.3cm) wider than your quilt top. If your quilt top is more than 32" (81.3cm) wide, you can sew two or more pieces of fabric together to make the quilt backing. Your quilt shop may also offer wide-back fabric, which is an alternative to piecing your backing fabric. Wide-back fabric is up to 108" (274.3cm) wide and can be cut to the desired length.

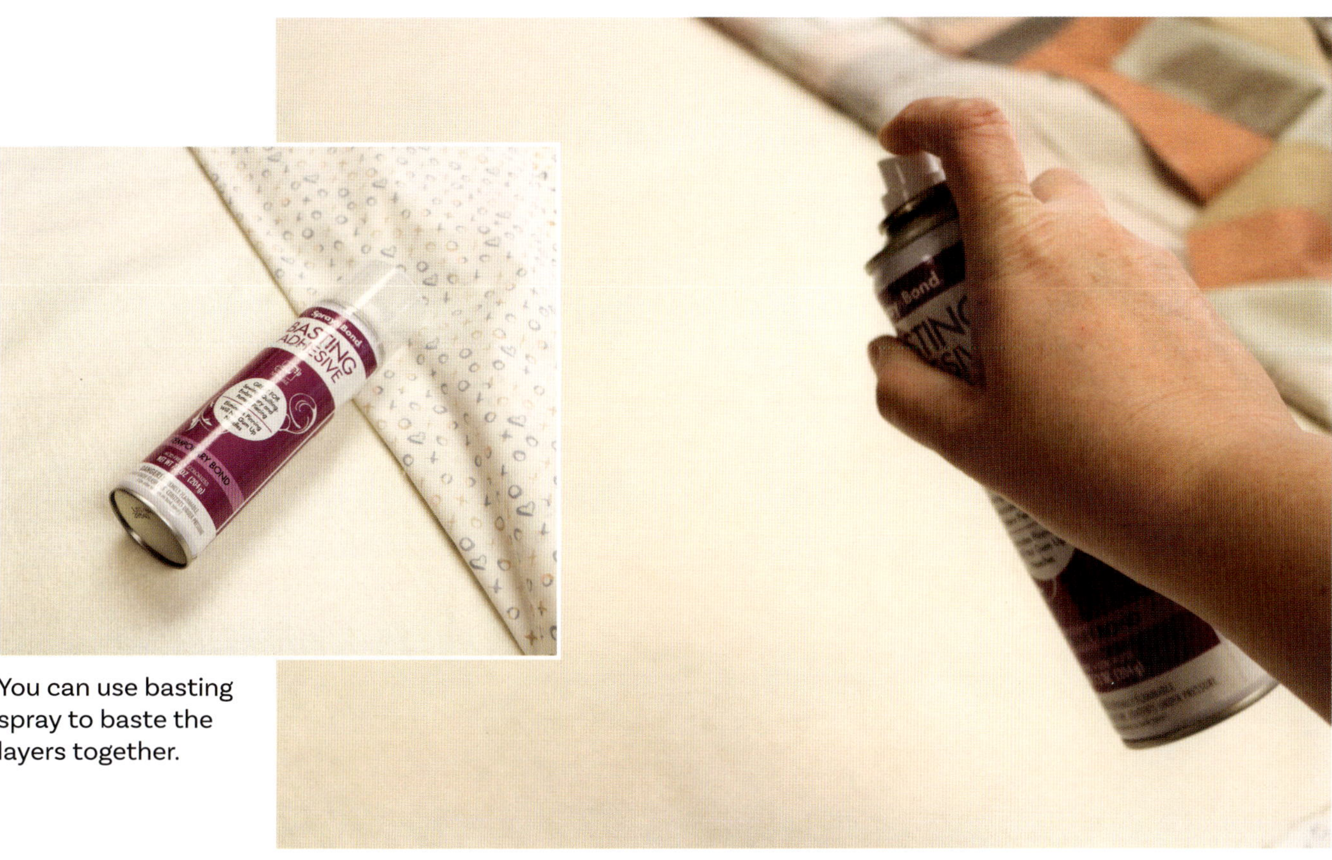

You can use basting spray to baste the layers together.

3. Cut your batting. Your batting should be about 6" (15.2cm) taller and 6" (15.2cm) wider than your quilt top.

4. Baste the three layers together. You can baste with pins or basting spray. Basting spray is often preferred because it is faster and less tedious. To spray baste your quilt, lay the batting on a large table or clean floor. Place the quilt top on top, right side up, centering it on the batting. Working one section at a time, lift the quilt top, spray the basting spray on the batting according to the manufacturer's instructions, and then gently place the quilt top down and press it into place.

5. Once the top is basted to the batting, flip it over so the quilt top is facing the table and the back of the batting is face up. Place the quilt backing on top of the batting. Repeat the process to spray baste the backing to the batting.

Quilting

Before stitching your quilt, make a plan. What kind of quilting design do you want? Will you quilt a horizontal and vertical grid? A crosshatched diagonal? Will you stitch-in-the-ditch or echo quilt next to the seams? You can quilt multiple parallel lines across the quilt vertically, horizontally, or diagonally.

Check the requirements on your batting for the maximum quilting distance. Depending on the type of batting, you may need to keep your quilting lines 8" (20.3cm) or less apart. You can have stitching that is closer together, but stitching that is farther apart will impact the longevity of your quilt.

1. Remove the foot from your sewing machine and replace it with a walking foot. The walking foot has feed dogs on the foot. This allows the quilt top and the quilt backing to feed through the sewing machine at the same rate, preventing shifting of the top relative to the backing.

2. Starting at one edge of the quilt, begin stitching on top of the quilt until you reach the other side.

3. Repeat, adding lines of quilting from one side to the other until it is fully quilted. Then, you are ready to trim up and bind your quilt.

Trimming Up

Trimming up your quilt is the process of trimming off the excess batting and backing fabric flush with the edges of the quilt top. A large ruler and cutting mat on a large table (or on a noncarpeted floor) will help you trim up your quilt.

1. Place the quilt top on top of your cutting mat. Using your largest ruler, start in one corner of the quilt. Line up the corner of the ruler with the corner of the quilt. Trim on both sides, along the edge of the ruler. Stop when you reach the end of your ruler, then reposition the ruler before you continue.

2. Go around the quilt, lining up the edge of the ruler with the edge of the quilt and trimming away the excess. You may find that the quilt top was not perfectly square or that it shifted in the quilting process. Squaring up the quilt is an opportunity to make small adjustments to bring the quilt edges back in line.

Binding

Binding is the process of finishing the edges of the quilt. There are many binding techniques. If you have a favorite binding technique, use that.

Binding strips are traditionally cut at 2½" (6.4cm), though some quilters prefer 2¼" (5.7cm) or 2" (5.1cm) binding strips. For these instructions, we'll focus on 2½" (6.4cm), binding because it is the most beginner friendly. The quilts in this book have all been bound with AGF 2.5 Edition, which is fabric specifically designed to be binding.

You can use bias-cut or straight-cut strips. Bias binding is the only option when binding curves or inset corners. When binding a traditional rectangle or square quilt, either option is fine. We'll focus on straight-cut binding for these instructions.

Binding is the process of finishing the edges of your quilt.

1. Measure all four sides of your quilt, then add these four numbers together. This is the perimeter of your quilt. Add 20" (50.8cm) to this number to give yourself enough binding for the corners and for joining your binding ends.

2. Divide this number by 40. This will tell you how many strips to cut.

3. Cut the required number of 2½" (6.4cm) strips.

4. Sew the strips together end-to-end on the diagonal. Sewing the strips on the diagonal reduces the bulk at the joined ends and prevents lumpy binding.

5. Trim the ends to a ¼" (6.4mm) seam allowance, then press the seams open. Pressing the seams open is also a measure taken against a lumpy seam allowance.

6. Press the binding in half, making a very long, narrow strip.

7. (Optional) Pin the binding to the quilt to ensure that no binding seams end up in the corners. The raw edges of the binding should line up with the raw edges of the quilt.

8. Stitch the binding to the front of the quilt, leaving at least a 5" (12.7cm) tail unstitched at your starting point. When you reach the corners, use a mitering technique as follows:

8a. Fold the binding at a right angle so that it moves away from the quilt.

8b. Fold the binding back so that the folded edge is against the edge of the quilt and the binding lines up with the edge of the quilt.

8c. Move the mitered corner out of the way. Stitch up to ¼" (6.4mm) from the edge. Lock your stitches.

8d. Cut the thread. Pivot the quilt 90° to stitch the next side. Move the mitered corner out of the way.

8e. Lock your stitches and begin stitching on the next side.

9. Just as you did at the beginning, you will stop stitching and leave at least 5" (12.7cm) of binding unstitched as you approach the end. Measure to ensure your binding, once attached, will lie flat, and join your binding strips together in an angled seam as shown in step 5. Press the seam open. Realign with the edge of the quilt, and finish stitching the binding.

10. Bring the binding to the back of the quilt. Stitch in place by hand or machine.

Acknowledgments

I'd like to thank the fabulous companies that support me, without whom this book would not be possible.

Thank you, Art Gallery Fabrics for the gorgeous fabrics shown on these pages. All quilts were made using AGF 10" Fabric Wonders and bound with AGF 2.5 Edition. The feel of these fabrics made working on this book a joy, and the colors and designs brought the quilts to life.

And a special thank you to Baby Lock, USA. I quilted all the quilts in this book myself on my Baby Lock machines. The majority of these quilts were quilted on my Baby Lock Gallant XL with Pro-Stitcher Lite. One was quilted on my Baby Lock Sashiko machine, and the walking foot quilting was done on my Baby Lock Ballad.

During the making of this book, I designed the Cake Cutter Ruler. It is designed specifically for making quilts from 10" squares, including all the quilts in this book.

About the Author

Carolina Moore started quilting over 30 years ago—before pre-cuts were invented! She first fell in love with pre-cuts when working at her local quilt shop. With a young child at home and one more on the way, making quilts with pre-cuts was a fast and easy way to make a quilt for a friend, a holiday, or just because.

Now that she runs a busy quilt pattern design and notions company in San Diego, California, pre-cuts are still a go-to for making quilts.

An award-winning quilter with a successful YouTube channel, Carolina Moore has designed notions to make sewing and quilting easier, including the Boxed Bag Template, the Diamond Strip Ruler, the Foundation Piecing Water Pen, and the Carolina Moore Glow Ruler. She loves making quilting faster, easier, and more accurate.

Check out Carolina Moore's other books: *Ultimate Paper Piecing Reference Guide* and *Sewing Perfect Little Bags and Totes.*

Index